TO LOVE AGAIN

Preparing the widowed and divorced for remarriage

By Duane and LeeAnn Rawlins

VMI Publishers
Sisters, OR

TrustedBooks

BOOKS YOU CAN DEPEND ON

a division of VMI Publishers
Sisters, Oregon
www.vmipublishers.com

ISBN: 1-933204-09-5
ISBN 13: 978-1-933204-09-3
Library of Congress Control Number: 2005935225

Author Contact: leeandee@juno.com
http://www.newlifeministries.com

We would like to dedicate this to all our dear friends and acquaintances who have been brave enough to risk remarriage after they experienced a painful departure of their first mate, either by death or divorce. And to our heavenly Father who is the only one able to restore us so that we can love again.

ACKNOWLEDGMENTS

WE ARE VERY APPRECIATIVE of the many people who, through their lives and wisdom, have contributed to the material in this book. We especially want to thank Scott and Sandi Tompkins for their significant contributions in concepts, content and editing. Without them this book may not have happened.

We belong to a writers group in Kona, Hawaii, and each member of that group has given us counsel, encouragement and feedback that have been most helpful. Also we would like to thank Barb Overgaard for her help with this project, and all those who endorsed our work.

And, last but not least, we want to give thanks and glory to our heavenly Father for His love and goodness to us in helping us to love again.

FOREWORD

IF THERE WAS EVER A TIME in the Body of Christ for a simple, straightforward, tell-it-like-it-is book for those who are re-entering the arena of matrimony, that time is now. As one who recently got married again after the death of my first wife, I can give solid testimony that the journey to love again is a wild and wonderful reality. Sometimes dangerous and fearsome even under the best of circumstances, this journey is well worth the taking, but requires significant help along the way.

One can scarcely begin to list the issues that confront those seeking to love again. Family patterns long established and seen as normal are suddenly exposed as dysfunctional and damaging. Relational styles that fit one situation no longer stand up in the face of new dynamics. Comfort zones become a thing of the past, and everything that matters about anything comes into question.

In my own situation, my new bride Marie and I have wrestled through all kinds of issues, ranging from how we process information to whether we prefer charcoal or propane grills, from simple issues like paint color to the shark-infested waters of relationships with children and grandchildren. When facing questions requiring deep wisdom such as the issue of financial holdings, the likes and dislikes of our sexual relationship, or what kind of living standard we will pursue, we have longed for the wisdom of those that have gone before us to help us come to the right conclusions. The fact that both of us have a strong and intimate relationship with Jesus Christ has been an overwhelming help to us, but even with that foundation a couple can struggle deeply with even the simplest issues facing those who dare to begin again in the adventure of romance.

Duane and LeeAnn Rawlins have answered the cry from those who need help in this matter in the volume that you hold in your hand. *To Love Again* is the nuts and bolts handbook that should be required reading for every couple contemplating this decision. Written with delightful candor and refreshing simplicity, this book is one that is desperately needed and greatly helpful. The Rawlins' have lived the things about which they write, and the book rings with the authority that comes when messengers and their message are congruent. Their romance is fresh and vibrant after nearly twenty years, and Marie and I have personally benefited from their counsel and prayers.

My prayer is that you will read this volume together with your new love, pray through the things that are addressed, and entrust yourselves into the hands of God Who loves you. Our God loves to build strength into the marriages of His children, and He delights in those who seek His will and His ways. You will be blessed, and your heart and soul will be strengthened for the journey ahead.

Gary Wiens
President, Burning Heart Ministries Inc.
In association with the International House of Prayer
Kansas City, Missouri

Contents

INTRODUCTION

THE WEDDING RESONATED with images of purity. Splashes of white orchids adorned the church from top to bottom. A virgin bride in a brilliant white gown and veil fairly danced to the altar in radiant joy. And vows bespoke a commitment to lifelong love, devotion, and holiness.

In entering a second marriage we may long for that glorious innocence. But we are no longer virgins in any sense of the word. We take our vows knowing full well the harder realities of marriage. And typically we bring to the altar baggage that we never had the first time around – fears, regrets, habit patterns, shattered dreams, unrealistic expectations, along with some emotional wounds, children, and/or financial problems.

No wonder it's so hard for couples to succeed in second marriages. The cold statistical reality is that 60 percent of second marriages fail, usually within the first ten years. The second hard reality for those remarrying after a divorce is that they are nearly twice as likely to divorce again as someone marrying after the death of a spouse.

All this adds up to one huge risk. So why marry again with the odds so stacked against us? Were it dependent on our own strength and wisdom, it wouldn't be worth the risk at all. But praise God that we don't have to rely on our own ability. We can overcome the odds by relying on the redeeming power of Jesus Christ. Yes, the same power that raised Jesus from the dead, that brought you to salvation, that gave you a future hope can help you overcome marriage challenges, too. Thousands of loving, happy, deeply committed second marriages testify to God's great power to heal and to merge two broken hearts into oneness. So yes, the risks are great, but the rewards are heavenly.

This book was written by two "wounded" people who gained the courage to love again through the redeeming power of Jesus Christ. We don't claim that our experiences are fully representative of today's divorced or widowed Christians. But we hope our experiences and those of dozens more second-marriage couples, who have helped us in the writing of this book, will help you or someone you love take the risk to love again. God created us with a need for love, and marriage is His most inspired model for giving and receiving love.

Duane and LeeAnn Rawlins were married November 27, 1986, and agree that they love their second marriage as much as the first. Both spouses from their first marriages died, and they took very different journeys to a new relationship. Duane currently is in his fourth "career" and says God has taught him much along the way. He served as an officer in the U.S. Navy and then worked for twenty-five years in the Los Angeles County school system, retiring as assistant superintendent of schools. Then he and his first wife Betty moved with their three children to Oregon, where he started a successful real estate business. Over the past twenty-five years, Duane has also taught all over the world in Youth With A Mission (YWAM), an interdenominational missions organization.

Despite these life successes, his world suffered a major blow in 1985 when Betty passed into eternity after a seven-year battle with cancer. Losing his precious wife after thirty-seven wonderful years of marriage shook everything in Duane's life: "I felt lost without her. So much of our lives was intertwined. I had to learn to deal with the pain and loneliness, and to let God fill that great empty place in my heart. I loved being married and I wanted to marry again, but I had a lot to learn to be ready. It took much effort and humility."

LeeAnn and her first husband Willard managed a large farm and manufacturing company near Harrisburg, Oregon. Together they raised three sons who all love the Lord. As committed Christians, both were active in their church and community. Their family was part of a singing ministry for eighteen years. They loved life and lived it to the fullest. Then came Willard's sudden and unexpected death from an aneurism on March 10, 1984.

"We were all devastated," recalls LeeAnn. "Only our strong faith in God pulled us through those first awful weeks. In the months that followed my husband's death, I took many baby steps and a few steps backwards. But God's faithfulness was demonstrated in many ways as I learned to take just one day at a time. Throughout all that pain, the Lord poured out His love on me and my family. He also gave me a greater compassion for others who are suffering.

"I remember one day being in a group of church friends who were ministering to me. Suddenly, from the corner of my eye, I caught a glimpse of a friend. Her husband had left her for another woman and filed for divorce. I caught myself gasping. No one was around her; no one was showing her affection. I knew she was in pain, too, but recognized that those who lose a spouse through a divorce do not have the same support as I did following a death. My heart broke so much over this, that in a few days I called my friend, asking her forgiveness because those of us who know His love were so insensitive. Insensitive because of our past training that if we embrace those who are divorced it will appear that we condone divorce. That is far from the truth!"

In losing a spouse to death or divorce, some issues are the

same but some are different. We have gleaned much insight and wisdom from many friends who also are in second marriages. We do not claim to have all the answers, but our research and the insights we have received from the Lord have been helpful to us and to others. We pray they will be to you as well. As you read let God speak to you and help you make your second marriage even better.

Chapter 1

REDEMPTION

Accepting God's intention

CHANCES ARE THAT you are reading this book because you are preparing to remarry or have already done so. You're excited, and yet deep down you're scared, too. You should be. Coming into a second marriage is a risky thing. According to U.S. Census statistics, 60 percent of second marriages fail and, if children are involved, the failure rate jumps to 70 percent. But it doesn't have to be that way.

God is in the business of redemption. He delights in taking our brokenness and turning it into something beautiful. Millions of successful second marriages are testimony to His faithfulness in helping Christian men and women through all the thorny issues they will face in a second marriage. Whether you have suffered the death of a spouse or been shattered by the pain and rejection of a divorce, God can fully prepare you to love again. Your willingness to let Him work on your heart is paramount to your success.

We believe most of these marriages fail because the marriage partners are not yet prepared to remarry. Many come into marriage with festering emotional wounds, wrong motives, unrealistic expectations and an attitude of denial about hot issues like finances, sex, location changes, and blended families. Every person wanting to marry again should look first at their motives. Are you merely looking for release from loneliness, the pain of death or divorce, guilt or shame? Or perhaps your motive is to gain more financial security or to get help in raising your children. It is not wrong to want these things, but if you're looking to a new spouse to fill all these needs you are putting him or her in the place of God, creating expectations that they can never fulfill. Marriage isn't a place to hide from the past. It's a partnership for the future. Marriage may temporarily satisfy many of your needs and desires, but if you have not dealt with the deeper issues in your life, it will provide only brief respite, not redemption.

The intimacy of marriage leaves little room for hiding. The personal issues that we have not taken to the cross before marriage will not remain hidden when "the two become one." To prepare for a second marriage, we must give room to the Redeemer to change conditions in our hearts that will be obstacles to physical, spiritual, and emotional intimacy in a second marriage.

In beginning His public ministry, Jesus declared, "[God] has sent me to bind up the brokenhearted, to proclaim freedom for the captives and release from darkness for the prisoners ..." (Isa. 61:1b). According to another prophecy of the Messiah's ministry, "A bruised reed he will not break, and a smoldering wick he will not snuff out. In faithfulness he will bring forth justice ..." (Isa. 42:3).

These words likely describe some of your own feelings about your life after losing your spouse – brokenhearted, imprisoned in darkness, bruised, and barely flickering. In these times of pain it is easy to turn our hurt and anger at God. Mistrust, fear, and bitterness grow when we blame God for our circumstances rather than drawing on His strength to overcome them.

You may be stuck because you are angry with your former mate. You may be afraid that you'll be left alone again. Or you may be bitter toward God for allowing your mate to die or to leave you.

These raw emotions seem to continually boil up within us after a divorce or death. They torment our minds and rip at our hearts. And if we let them simmer they will eventually surface in ways that tear apart our relationships, especially our relationship with God. To be ready for a second marriage, we must be willing to lay down any remaining anger, fear, or bitterness, and to let Jesus cover it with His blood.

To some of us this is a blind spot. It is hard for us to see these attitudes, much less do something about them. That is why we all need some kind of premarital counseling. Whether it is done by a licensed marriage counselor, a pastor, or a wise Christian friend, we need to be challenged about areas we can't see or are unwilling to address. We need encouragement to forgive ourselves for past failures in marriage, to forgive our previous spouse for wounds caused to us or our children, to forgive people who have betrayed our confidence or given bad counsel, and to acknowledge and receive forgiveness for any anger we still harbor toward God. Yes, this is difficult and it may seem impossible, but no wound or sin is too big for God's healing grace. Only by dealing head-on with our pain and bitterness can we enter a second marriage with any hope of success.

The question of divorce

In writing this book we do not wish to imply that losing a spouse through divorce is the same as losing one through death. At most weddings we make "until death do us part" promises. If we are Christians, these are more than just promises. They represent a covenant before God—an eternal relationship in which we trust God to help us fulfill the promises of this lifetime commitment.

If we remain faithful until our spouse's death, then we have honored our promises, and we are free to enter a new relationship (1 Cor. 7:39).

In divorce, we break those promises, and God is grieved. "I hate divorce," says the LORD God of Israel in Malachi 2:16. He hates divorce because it tears lives apart and shatters trust. Obviously, it is much harder to enter a second marriage because of that.

Does this mean that a divorced person will always have a broken relationship with God and therefore be unsuccessful in a second marriage? Absolutely not! The blood of the cross is big enough to cover even divorce. The church, to its shame, sometimes treats divorced people as if they have committed an unforgivable sin. But that doesn't mesh with the gospel of grace. In addressing the Pharisees, Jesus spoke firmly against divorce when addressing their question, "Is it lawful for a man to divorce his wife for any and every reason?" (Matt. 19:3). But in Matthew 5:32, he recognized "marital unfaithfulness" as a reason for divorce. In 1 Corinthians 7:12-15, the Apostle Paul notes another exception. "If any brother has a wife who is not a believer and she is willing to live with him, he must not divorce her. And if a woman has a husband who is not a believer and he is willing to live with her, she must not divorce him... But if the unbeliever leaves, let him do so. A believing man or woman is not bound in such circumstances; God has called us to live in peace."

Through the centuries, millions of unbelievers have been led to faith in Christ by the witness of their spouses. God wants us to pray for them and to love them in the manner of 1 Corinthians 13. But if they cannot abide your faith and choose to leave, then you are "not bound."

We believe there is another exception that also represents the heart of God as we know it from the scriptures. We believe He would not have a spouse stay in a relationship with a mate who has a pattern of life-threatening violence toward her/him or their children. As Paul says, "God has called us to live in peace."

Our friend Brian believes that his decades-long marriage to Michelle represents in many ways God's redemptive power in divorce. He recalls, "I was 21 when I married a bright, attractive woman (we'll call her Jeannie) who was a college classmate. I knew she had a troubled past, but I thought I could be the answer to her problems. Within a year of our wedding day, however, she was again pursuing other men. When I discovered her unfaithfulness, I was crushed. She left and my world fell apart. I always imagined I would have a long marriage like my parents. The thought of divorce left me in despair.

"But it was out of that shattering experience that I opened my heart to Christ. His love flooded into my life and changed everything. One of the changes was a budding relationship with Michelle, a co-worker who received Christ about the same time. I had been separated from my wife for nearly a year, but I was still not divorced. As Michelle and I began to fall in love and talk about marriage, we both sensed that God wanted me to try again to reconcile my marriage. Both of us were willing to sacrifice our relationship to obey God's Word in this (1 Cor. 7:12). Therefore I reached out to Jeannie again. As we spent time together she said she regretted what had happened, but doubted she could ever be faithful. I told her again of the forgiveness and newness of life I had received from Jesus. When she rejected these offers, I was sad for her sake, but I felt free in my spirit.

"Michelle and I will always be thankful that after we married, we became part of a church that understood the power of grace and redemption. Like others who had been divorced, we were discipled in the ways of God and then affirmed and encouraged as we rose in ministry and leadership within the church. For more than 35 years now we have served in positions of leadership. What a loss to the church if we and others had been told that our divorces precluded us from ever being fully accepted by God and fit for ministry. Yet this happens all the time. Yes, God hates divorce, and we who have been divorced need to raise the standard against it. But He loves the people who have been through this awful experience. He not only wants to fully equip them for fruitfulness in ministry, He wants to prepare many for a second marriage, a marriage in which He is honored and glorified."

Facing a "root issue" before remarriage

As we consider the problems we've had in both our first and second marriages, it becomes obvious that most stem from selfishness and pride. *These trials come straight from our old carnal (human) nature which Paul, the apostle, refers to as the flesh.*

Duane spent thousands of hours trying to train his old nature to be kind, loving, patient, and gracious – all to no avail. After twenty-five years of marriage he began to realize that behind all of his marital issues was this fleshly nature that would not change. He finally realized that he needed to put it to death, that this is a conscious choice he must make daily – a choice to submit his will to God's.

Paul says in Romans 8:13, "I die daily." As he began to die daily to his old nature instead of trying to fix it, he began to see big changes in his marriage and many other areas of his life. This is a critical step for people going into second marriages. We have often learned to be tough and self-reliant to get through the loss of our spouses, so learning to submit our will to God and another person doesn't come easily. Paul reminds us that it is only though the help and power of the Holy Sprit that this crucifixion of our flesh is possible.

If you are struggling with selfishness, pride, and other issues of the flesh, you don't want to take these into a new marriage. Invite the Holy Spirit into your life and ask Him to lead you every day. As the Apostle Paul said in Romans 8:14, "[T]hose who are led by the Spirit of God are sons of God." Those who are led by the Spirit are also the ones who will be successful in a second marriage.

Tuning into the Father's voice

Amid all the pain and turmoil of a death or divorce, many people lose their ability to be sensitive to the voice of God. Some never had it to begin with. Restoring this openness to the Holy Spirit's voice is another key to success in a second marriage and in life itself. God says to wait upon Him. We must take time to listen if we ever expect to hear His voice.

King David learned this lesson well and declared in Psalm 38:15, "I wait for you, O LORD; you will answer, O Lord my God." We can have that same certainty. If we take our concerns and questions to God and then pause to listen, He will answer. Psalm 37:7 says, "Be still before the LORD and wait patiently for Him."

Have you learned to do this in your everyday life? When you invite the Holy Spirit to guide you and are quick to obey, you may be amazed at how clear His direction becomes on many issues.

Once LeeAnn was driving with her four-year-old granddaughter, and she was talking about someone that she was going to go help move. "Why are they moving away?" her granddaughter asked. "They feel God is telling them to move there," she replied. Her little granddaughter cocked her head to the side, looked at LeeAnn with her big brown eyes and said, "Nanny,

God doesn't speak to people." Lee Ann said, "You know, honey, we don't usually hear His voice out loud, but often we have a sense in our heart about what He is saying to us." She looked at LeeAnn, and then out the window and said, "Hum, it must be too noisy at my house."

Could it be that it is often too noisy at many houses to hear what He has to say?

One key to hearing God is to come to Him in faith, expecting an answer. God communicates in various ways, and foremost among them is the Bible, His written Word. God wants us to search the Scriptures, for His truths about all the major issues of life are spoken to us through the Bible. He may also speak to us through an inner voice (Isa. 30:21), an audible voice (Ex. 3:4), through dreams (Matt. 2) and visions (Rev. 1:12-17). Allow God to speak to you in the manner He chooses. Receive your own leading, when asking for guidance. Other godly people may confirm your guidance, but don't look to others to give it to you.

In his book *Is That Really You, God?* Youth With A Mission founder Loren Cunningham says, "Practice hearing God's voice and it becomes easier. It's like picking up the phone and recognizing the voice of your best friend. Don't make guidance complicated. It's actually hard NOT to hear God if you really want to please and obey Him."[1]

Trusting in His character

Another thing that often gets shattered in a death or divorce is our basic trust in God's good intentions for our lives. We can read passages like Jeremiah 29:11 that declare the Lord's plans to do us good. But when life-shaking events occur, that foundation can be eroded or torn asunder. Our understanding of the Father must be based on a rock-solid belief that He cares for us and that

He will use every circumstance in life, even the seemingly bad ones, for our good if we will trust Him.

Many of us can quote Romans 8:28: "And we know that in all things God works for the good of those who love Him, who have been called according to His purpose." How many of us live in expectation that all the challenges of our lives will turn out for our good?

There was a Chinese farmer who had a great black stallion. One day it ran away, and the neighbors gathered around and exclaimed, "This is awful!" The Chinese farmer replied, "We cannot judge. It could be for our good. We have to wait and see." In a few days the stallion returned and brought ten healthy mares into the corral. In the weeks that followed, the farmer's son was trying to break one of the mares and he fell off and broke his leg and arm. The neighbors gathered around again and said, "This is terrible!" The farmer replied kindly, "It seems bad, but we must wait and see." In a few days, a Chinese warlord came and conscripted all the town's able-bodied young men for battle. Because his son had a broken leg and arm, he did not have to go.

The point is that we don't always see the big picture. In God's great redemptive way He will turn our sorrows into avenues of blessing. We would not wish the pain of a divorce or a spouse's death on anyone. However, as we have come through these dark valleys with faith, He has taught us things about His character and ways that have become tools to help others. He will do that for you, too, if you will continually trust in His love and good intentions for you.

LeeAnn admits that she did question God's promise in Romans 8:28 during the days and weeks following the death of her wonderful husband Willard. They had enjoyed a holiday together at the Oregon coast celebrating her 43rd birthday two weeks earlier. Little did she realize that it would be their last holiday together. Willard awoke that rainy morning looking the picture of good health. But an aneurism burst in his chest, and his life ebbed away in seconds.

None of us has any guarantees about life or how long we will be married. We never know what tomorrow will bring. When Willard died, LeeAnn did not know how she would ever go on alone. Those first years, especially, were lonely and bleak. She loved God and daily experienced His faithfulness, but she needed time to heal. She was not sure if she could ever remarry, or if she even wanted to. She loved Willard so much.

In time God did redeem and restore. LeeAnn would have told you in those days that it would take a miracle for her to ever be truly happy again. But God performs miracles every day, and her second marriage to Duane is one of them. As author Ann Graham Lotz says so well in *Just Give Me Jesus*, "Ours is the God of the second chance, the slim chance, and the no chance!" There is no redeemer like Jesus.

One of the many people we interviewed for this book – a woman named Susan – is one of those examples of redemption. She was the "other woman" in an affair that broke up both marriages and brought her to the brink of suicide. She had no convictions about divorce one way or the other. Every move she made was motivated by selfishness; she wanted what she wanted when she wanted it.

At the time, Susan was twenty-five and had been married for three years. She wasn't unhappy, she explained, she and her husband had just grown apart. After the divorce, one affair led to another. For the next five years, Susan lived a swinging single life, but she was miserable. She thought she'd never be able to love or be loved again. Then she met Jesus. As she repented in tears and committed her life to Him, He transformed her. She settled down with a fine Christian man and has been happily married for eighteen years.

God's pathway to freedom

Unfortunately, there are millions of men and women who, like Susan, have messed up their lives and think they could never love again. Because of their frailties and failures they believe they are unworthy of God's love and the love of a prospective spouse. They let this lie keep them from embracing God's redemptive power and the blessings He intends for them.

If this describes you – if God is giving you another chance at love and marriage, don't be afraid. Embrace it. Submit yourself to God and let His redemptive power prepare you to love again. The Hebrew word for redemption, *padah*, refers to a release from an undesirable condition affected by someone who paid the price as the redeemer. Redemption in the Old Testament was broad, including the buying back of people from slavery or buying back property. It is also used in the general sense of the deliverance of Israel as a nation from the slavery of Egypt and other bondage.

The redemption needed in the *spiritual and physical realms* from undesirable human conditions became the analogy by which the Hebrew people could understand their eternal condition of bondage and the need for redemption of soul and spirit. Redemption is a release from the effects and power of sin and a restoration of the relationship between God and man as originally intended. In the Garden of Eden, prior to the entrance of sin (choosing one's own way versus dependence on and obedience to a Holy God), the relationship between God and humans was close and pure. He wants not only to restore that intimate relationship between us and Him, but also to enable us to have healthy, whole, intimate relationships with one another.

Jesus has already paid the price for our redemption, and that includes restoring our hearts, healing our hurts, and delivering us from those things (bondages) that are obstacles to our moving on into the abundant lives He has for us, with or without a new partner and soul mate. We can't pay any more than Jesus has already paid, but we can walk into the freedom that He has secured for us by choosing to agree with Him, and by choosing to hand over to Him our "undesirable condition." In this very act of allowing Him to "cut us loose" from the grief, anger, and hurt caused by death, abuse, or even our own actions, we are on the road to restoration!

Chapter 2

CHANGE

A MOTHER SENT HER SON out to pick some wild berries. The boy took nothing in which to carry the berries. You can imagine the condition of the berries when the boy emptied his pocket onto the table. His mother said, "Where is your common sense? The next time I send you to get something for me, have the presence of mind to carry it home in a box."

As the story goes, two days later she sent him to a friend's house to find his four-year-old brother who was visiting there . . . I'll bet you have already guessed the punch line. The older brother returned home with his little brother kicking and screaming inside a big cardboard box.

Sometimes we all need to be reminded that the methods that worked yesterday may not help us out today or tomorrow. Life changes, circumstances change. People change.

In this chapter we want to help you see that change can be good. One of the greatest mistakes we can make is to be inflexible and resist change. "Therefore if any man be in Christ, he is a new creature: old things are passed away: All things are become new" (2 Cor. 5:17).

When we move out of marriage by death or divorce we move into a new season. Whether we like it or not our lives have been changed. Nothing in Duane and LeeAnn's lives was more devastating than watching the men from the funeral parlor place their loved ones in black bags and carry them away, never to be seen again here on earth. Their lives had been significantly altered and nothing they could do would bring the loved ones back.

Change never comes easily. We need to be aware that there are all kinds of forces attempting to keep us from changing. One of the primary forces is our enemy the devil. He wants to keep us looking back, yearning for yesterday. It's very difficult to let go and step into a new thing, a new tomorrow, especially when it is unclear what tomorrow will bring. Often God will ask us to let go of something without revealing what's on the other side of His request.

Duane tells about change in his life

Duane was moving into a season of darkness and loneliness. Betty, his wife, was seriously ill and the dreaded day crept upon them. He thought he was prepared but, looking back, nothing can fully prepare you for the awfulness of losing your life partner. His family and friends were kind and loving but no one could replace the intimacy and love they shared.

Duane's life was very different. He knew he had to change. He could fight it, tolerate it, or celebrate it. This was not easy; it took months for him to get his head screwed on right. He thought he was normal in his thought process but it was still very painful. It seems that one of the first thoughts he experienced was, "Why me, Lord?" He took some time to try to get a clearer picture of the fact that we all die sooner or later and it is extremely unusual for a husband and wife to pass away at the same time.

Suddenly, he was being pushed out of his comfort zone and he did not like it. Betty had done a great job of taking care of his daily needs. Now he was responsible for providing his meals, washing his clothes, and cleaning his house. He prayed daily for God's mercy. He drank liberally from His grace.

Widowerhood had brought about many changes that, at this stage, he was only tolerating.

Duane had always enjoyed working, studying, and teaching so he poured himself into each of these areas. He began to travel more and teach in various locations around the world.

When he was alone, usually at night, he still found himself very lonely and only tolerating change. It was while teaching in Singapore at the Youth With A Mission base that he decided it was time to make significant changes in his life. It was time to stop tolerating and, instead, to start celebrating change.

In this chapter we would like to share what we have learned from research and personal experience about change.

Change requires us to move out of our comfort zone, and there are natural roadblocks that cause us to want to back up and stay where we are. Fear of the unknown raises its ugly head. We find ourselves in unfamiliar surroundings with new and different people, and this causes us to be unsure as to what to say and do.

Most every major change in life involves some degree of loss. But seldom is the loss as great as when you lose your mate to death.

Was it really possible that God still had a rich full life for Duane to live? Out of these ashes could he find new blessings? Would he experience joy and happiness in his senior years? It had been almost a year since Betty died and he was beginning to realize that his life was changing, and for the most part it was good.

There were new mountains to move, new relationships to develop, books to write and maybe even a new partner to enjoy life with. He prayed and sought God for the qualities that he would want in a new mate. He gave Duane his heart's desire by bringing LeeAnn Smucker into his life. Her husband had died a little over two years before. They spent time together and began to realize that they had much in common and much to celebrate.

How change came into LeeAnn's life

Her husband of twenty-four years, Willard, whom she loved very much, died suddenly of an aneurism in his chest. In a matter of a few minutes her wonderful world fell apart. She was a widow just two weeks after her forty-third birthday. Her head swam with thoughts of the changes in her world that this awful moment would bring. Changes she did not want to deal with.

LeeAnn shifted from being a housewife and mother with a shared parenting role, to being a full-on businesswoman and single mom. How grateful she was that she had assisted Willard in their businesses before his death. This helped her carry on the businesses. But to have the full responsibility of running them – that was a big change. Also how was she to manage as a single parent? The list went on and on. In that one moment her life changed in many ways. Some changes she felt she might never be able to deal with. She loved being a team player and the thought of going on alone was almost unbearable.

God was faithful and provided many ways to help LeeAnn deal with her new life. As she looks back she marvels at how He helped her in many different ways. It was in the second year, after that fateful day, that God brought Duane Rawlins into LeeAnn's life. Her marriage to Duane brought still another change, a good change, but one that would not always be easy.

Often, in the initial stage, a situation might look bad. It feels bad and from every side it's hard to swallow. Here is where we need to take a deep breath and be willing to change. When trouble comes, remember this: it came to pass – it didn't come to stay. See it as a chance to be yourself; enjoy life as you stumble through it. Even if you fall, God is always there to pick you up.

Divorce brings change

Since we knew only what it was like to be left alone through the death of our mate, we needed to glean some examples of others who found change in their lives through divorce. Those examples follow.

About a year after each divorced, Sally and Joe married. They shared with us how this affected them as change came about in their lives.

It was not very long before they found they were very different people. This underlined the need for change in both their lives. Sally said, "I had spent many years doing everything my way and being a type "A," do-it-right-away-type person. Joe also had been used to doing things his way and was always careful to take plenty of time to make a full study before deciding on things. We both came to realize that this difference could work to our advantage if we prayed about each decision and were willing to change."

They told us as a way to help them remember to defer to each other, on the inside of their wedding rings they had engraved first "God," then their spouse's name, and then their own name. With that order in mind, it became a privilege to defer to each other, and change was made easier.

How change affected other couples

Jane had been married to Bill, who did things on the spur of the moment. Jane said, "I learned early in our marriage that plans could change, I adjusted to that, and enjoyed this quality in him. But other serious problems developed that led to our divorce.

"Several years later I met Jim. He was a great guy, but I realized that he was rigid. Plans were made and not changed.

This bothered me and Jim was equally bothered by my being so changeable with plans. We both thought, 'Oh this will change, we will help each other.' After we were married, the situation only got worse. Neither one of us wanted to change our view. Finally, after much heartache, we decided we needed help. We went to a counselor and received guidance. Things did not get better overnight, but we each learned to give a little. After we both worked hard for several months, we saw progress beginning to take place. Change is hard, but don't buck it. It is a great character builder."

Shirley and Robert wrote, "Most of the difficulties in the rather rocky early years of our marriage were a product of the wounds from our previous marriages. Neither of us had been healed from our rejection. Shirley had experienced the deep pain of infidelity. About the same time she was made aware of the fact that her father had been unfaithful in his marriage. This made trusting men very difficult. If I glanced at another woman or had a conversation that lasted too long, it stirred up all the old painful memories, and led her to question my motives. Why would I do those things when I knew how painful it was for her? None of the things I did were intentionally meant to hurt her, but were nevertheless, very insensitive.

"This was incredibly painful and frustrating for both of us," Robert continued. "She would question me relentlessly, and I would try to justify my behavior. We would then begin bitter verbal exchanges that wounded each other even more. I remember reflecting many times on the fact that before we married I desired to be a blessing to her and help make up for all the rejection she had experienced. Now, ironically, I was causing her more pain. All this anger and words about divorce that our daughters witnessed made them fearful of the possible outcome.

"We should have recognized how dangerous our problem

was, and what a tremendous threat it posed to our marriage and family. We didn't see how we could afford ongoing professional counseling. The type of counseling we needed never took place. There were times when I felt that if we would just seek God, His wisdom would be sufficient. But somehow that never happened, because I wasn't open to seeking God with my whole heart, no matter the cost. We ended up settling for a few brief sessions of pastoral counseling. I don't think anyone who counseled us ever knew how deep-seated and serious our problem was. It seems we were stuck, neither of us willing to change."

Suggestions for coping with change

As we read the above stories we see what can happen if we are not willing to deal with change.

We would like to offer you some suggestions that have helped us deal with change in our lives. For many of us, earlier mistakes that we have not taken care of have caused us to get stuck. We have pushed them down into our subconscious minds. As a defense mechanism, we refuse to deal with them. When they surface we push them back down again, hoping that over time they will go away, but they do not. In fact, they often return to haunt us. After several years, bondage sets in. We find ourselves being governed by these grudges, hurts and grievances. It is time to be set free. Propose in your heart to let God set you completely free. Give up your desire for revenge. See change as your friend.

Duane decided if he was going to enjoy this new life together with LeeAnn, it was time to stop pretending that he was someone he was not. He needed to be real and admit he was weak and inadequate. He made mistakes and needed to admit his shortcomings and be honest. After all, it is God's goodness and mercy that make the difference in us. It became clear to him that when he was wrong he just needed to admit it and ask for forgiveness. It always amazed him how quickly things cleared up. They both marveled at what a difference it made in their relationship when they agreed they didn't always have to be right. They began to encourage and support each other and not always worry about who was right.

Begin to forgive

We have mentioned forgiveness as a major action to take if you're going to move on in life. It restores our energy to move forward. Forgiveness is how you stop the pain.

Several years ago we were conducting a marriage retreat. A young couple, Jack and Alice, attended the retreat that weekend. They were on the verge of a breakup. This was to be their last-ditch effort to restore their marriage. Of course we did not know all the history that led to this crisis. However, they were convicted at the retreat. Alice said, "I know it is wrong but I am seeing another man. I love the gifts and attention he gives me." How easy it is to be led into sin when we are unhappy. Because they felt convicted, and because they had a little son they both loved, they decided to come to us for counseling. In the weeks that followed we spent time with them, individually and together.

Jack, the husband, was so hurt by the affair that it was hard for him to forgive. But during our counseling God gave Jack a revelation that He was no better than the man who was having an affair with Alice because he had sex with Alice before they were married. Jack had asked the Lord for forgiveness, but never Alice. So he went to Alice and asked for forgiveness. It touched Alice's heart so much that she broke off with the other man and she in turn asked Jack to forgive her for being involved with someone else. It was hard for Jack but he chose to forgive her for the affair. That day they began to rebuild their marriage on a solid foundation of forgiveness. Today, years later, they have a wonderful marriage. God has blessed them with more children and they are so grateful they made the choice to forgive and go on together.

If we do not forgive it grows into bitterness and affects everyone. It erupts in anger, and this anger can bring disease, stress and pain. Forgiveness calls us to grow in character, which is most pleasing to God.

Do you want to be bitter or better?

Jack could have chosen to hold on to un-forgiveness and let bitterness set in but he chose to forgive. How much better his life has been because of making the right choice to forgive.

Jack could have said, "You don't know how badly she hurt me." The truth is forgiveness is how you stop the pain.

As for both of us, before we met each other, it seemed it would be much easier to hold on to our bitterness and fill our days with complaints of how awful it was that we had lost our mates so young. But as we looked around, it wasn't long until we noticed others who were far worse off than we were. We decided it was time to start counting our blessings, take our focus off our past, and begin looking for the good around us. It was then that our world around us began to look better. This is a choice we need to make when we find ourselves in the middle of an undesirable situation.

One small thing that LeeAnn did was to start writing in a journal about the things that were helping her get through these hard times. She called it her "Bear It" book. Writing this was helpful to her. On days when she just could not find anything to write in her book, she would look back at all the good things she had written in the past days and months, which helped encourage her. Then one of her friends said she needed to write an "ugly book" to deal with the ugly things that were going on in her life during this time. Her friend brought her a little book with an ugly picture on it. She wrote down those ugly things in that book. Then she did not look back at them again. She found she needed to deal with those "ugly" things but not dwell on them. Recording these things helped her release those thoughts that were not good and keep bitterness from settling in her heart.

Remember, the only difference between bitter and better is the letter "i." Bitterness is like swallowing a bottle of poison and hoping the other person will die.

Dare to dream

Not long after we were married we decided we were ready to dream again and get on with life. We realized that it was time to clarify our dreams and be sure that God was in them. What were the desires of our hearts? It was not long before we had more clarity. We knew we wanted to touch lives, expand the kingdom, and leave this world a better place than we found it. As we thought about it, we realized that much of our personal growth had come from reading the Bible and other good books. We decided we would write more books. To date we have authored or co-authored nine books. These books are one way we have lived out our dreams. What are your dreams? Dream together and ask God to give you ways to make your dreams reality.

Many of us feel that there just isn't enough time to walk out our dreams. The truth is, we all have exactly the same amount of time. What we can do is avoid procrastinating. We must prioritize our activities. Learn the one thing that is most important in our lives. Know what needs to be done today and do it. We have a wonderful opportunity to make a difference as we move through life together. If we take this seriously, we will have a better marriage.

Celebrate change

We did not do everything right but we committed ourselves to celebrating changes in our lives and not just tolerating them. Things like where we would live, teach, what church to attend, and the list goes on. We wish we could say it was easy but it was not. Many days were sad and lonely. It was only our faith in God that brought us through. If you find yourself in the place of change because of death or divorce, lean into Him and trust Him. He will make a way. It is absolutely imperative that we allow these transitions in our life if we are going to reach our destiny. God has an unconditional guarantee that He will make everything work for good for those who love Him. He gives grace to the humble. His grace is sufficient.

Chapter 3

FILLING THE VOID

THERE ARE NOT WORDS big enough or strong enough to express the feeling you get when you lose your mate. Losing your mate to death is one of the most devastating experiences a person endures. To lose the one who knows you backward and forward, the one with whom you have shared many memories, creates many problems, but loneliness requires the hardest adjustment.

During this grieving process you find yourself denying the reality of death; you feel like it is a bad dream from which you will awaken. After a spouse dies, the world is a different place. It is emptier, lonelier, and less meaningful.

Being widowed causes loneliness. The clue to loneliness can be found in the line from Psalm 142: "No man cared for my soul" (v. 4, KJV). Loneliness makes you feel deserted and alone. Feeling lonely is like being isolated, even though others are close at hand. We know what it feels like when a mate dies, as do some of you who are reading this book. Others know the great void after losing a mate through divorce.

How do you fill that void? As a widow and widower, we know you hate that emptiness and feel that the only way to fill it is to get that deceased mate back. But, of course, that is not possible. Therefore, you start looking to find a way to fill this void. First let's look at things that do not work when trying to fill this void.

Staying busy

An adequate defense mechanism that works for a short while is to keep yourself busy with a great deal of activity. This may seem like a good way to avoid the pain but over time can create health problems or, at best, wear you out. You will become exhausted and suffer burnout. You may become so tired that rest is not even possible. You toss and turn and then wake feeling like a train ran over you. None of this helps you discover lasting wholeness. While being busy is not bad, staying too busy is hurtful. We found that being busy is good for the moment but it is only a temporary relief. The void is still there.

Forms of abuse

Another easy way to create short-term release from the pain and sorrow is to use alcohol and drugs to alleviate the hurt. This is a very poor form of escape that may damage your emotional and mental health. When the effects of drugs or alcohol wear off you find yourself in even greater pain. Drugs and alcohol can become very addictive if abused. Be aware of the trap you can find yourself in with substance abuse. Guilt and remorse are added to the loss and depression. This can happen so innocently with prescription drugs. If used inappropriately or abused, they can damage your health and well-being, only making your problems worse.

Some have chosen to use food as a form of relief. Again, if abused, you can find yourself overweight, which can create serious self-worth issues, physical appearance problems, and can lead to health problems. All this can further complicate your situation.

These forms of abuse have no power to help resolve the situation and usually make matters worse.

The sexual trap

Loneliness can cause us to jump into relationships and sexual activities that give only temporary relief at best. As Christians, we know that sex outside of marriage is sin. On top of this, it causes us to feel unfulfilled. Again, guilt sets in, making us even more miserable and lonely.

Since we have been married, we are more vulnerable because sexuality has been a very integral part of our lives. We both were very aware of our weakness and temptation in this area and tried to bend over backward to avoid any form of intimate contact (such as kissing or petting) during our time of singleness. We know that the safest way to avoid sinning is to avoid every situation that could lead one astray. Rather than seeing ourselves as strong, we chose to run away from all opportunities that could prove hazardous to our staying pure. We must keep in mind that our bodies are God's temple. We glorify God through proper care and use of them. They are a gift from Him, entrusted to us to use for His glory. Sex outside of marriage does not bring glory to Him.

Going from one relationship to another

When we move from one relationship to another, that awful vacuum is still there.

We must look to the Lord for our fulfillment, not man.

Life is not about playing games, especially when those "games" are harmful to another person.

George told us about his trying to fill this void by going in and out of relationships. Here is his story: "I had a wonderful wife whom I loved very much, I thought we were a happily married couple who were committed to loving each other and remaining faithful for as long as we both should live. However, she had different ideas. She entered into an adulterous relationship and soon decided she wanted out of our marriage. I was crushed. I felt that I would never trust again. I was in and out of relationships. Just as soon as it seemed to be more then just friendship, I was gone. I was sure that if I gave my heart away again, it would be crushed and broken, just like the first time. I realized I needed to get some help to get to the bottom of my inability to trust. These short relationships just were not filling that void in my heart. It took two years of godly counseling before I could get to the bottom of my problem. It has helped, but trusting is still hard for me. However, with God's help, I am learning to be an 'overcomer.'

We have been looking at what does not fill the vacuum in our lives, and now we want to look at what it takes to fill that void in positive ways.

Intimacy with the Lord

Our primary concern must be our relationship with the Lord. He will never leave us or forsake us. We know this is true in our head but do we really believe this in our hearts?

LeeAnn remembers how often she heard the trite line, "Honey, you just need to let Jesus be your husband." She remembers telling Jesus, "I love you so much and appreciate you for being there for me but you have created me to need skin." She remembers smiling and she knew He understood. She felt He was smiling, too. It is interesting, as she looks back, to see the many times Jesus truly was her husband, helping her with things in her business and with life's challenges.

He knew she needed "skin," but the greatest problem is when we look to that "skin" to bring us fulfillment that only the Lord can give.

A very important key here is found in John 10:10, where Jesus said, "I have come that they may have life and that they might have it abundantly."

Focus on helping others

Seek to serve and not to keep focusing on "poor me." When we reach out to others, we become more fulfilled. We must die to our flesh. We need to give ourselves to helping others. We look for ways to do this. Choose to visit someone in a nursing home or hospital. Take a friend, who is hurting, out to lunch or coffee. When we take our focus off our own hurts and loneliness, it brings healing to us. It often brings to our attention that there are others out there hurting, too. Sometimes just being with another person who hurts enables us to help each other. It often amazes us to see how God uses these situations to ease our own pain.

Recently we were very touched by the actions of a friend of ours. She had lost her husband seven years ago. She was left to raise four young children. Most of her time and energy went into making a living and raising her children. She taught school and gave herself to the children of her class.

In the midst of this she contracted cancer. With chemo treatment, and all that entails, she was still able to teach full time. Now comes the good part. She looked after an older widow. When this widow, Mary, broke her hip, our friend took time to stop by to see Mary every other day to love and support her friend. It was a wonderful example of someone who had had a very difficult life rising above it and reaching out to help someone in need. Needless to say, she has raised four wonderful young adults because she modeled love for her children.

Reach out by remembering the day others lost their mate. Take them to dinner, send a card, or just call. There is such comfort in someone sharing your pain. The beauty of this is how much it helps ease your own pain. Those who study personal behavior have discovered the "me too" approach often brings the brightest ray of hope to a hurting person.

LeeAnn remembers that when her husband died, she received many cards, letters, and many other acts of kindness during the first year. God opened up the windows of heaven and poured down His love on her. Receiving all this kindness surely did teach her that we are His hands and His feet. When you hear that small voice telling you to do something for someone who is hurting, don't wait or think it is too small and unimportant. What a joy it is if we listen and then do what He asks. She remembers so well a friend who called her from Kansas and said, "Oh, Lee-Ann, I just called to say I do not know what to say." Sometimes we say too much. Other times we keep to ourselves too much. Those few words touched her heart so much; these were just the words she needed.

When God is urging us, it is because He knows just what someone needs.

Learning to be content

We should work at being content with who we are. We should look inward and find the person God created us to be. We know that some of us just feel more complete when we have a mate, but it is important that we first find contentment with who we are. We found that until we became completely content with Him, He could not bring to us the person He had for us. If we are not content with who we are, we become very needy. Being overly needy creates a whole new set of problems. So work at being content with the person God made you to be. Rest in Him. Psalm 46:10 says, "Be still and know that I am God." Being still and listening is hard. It seems that too many of us talk to God, but too few listen to Him.

Often healing comes when we are one-on-one with God. This is not the easiest but often the most needed.

Waiting for His timing is important. Waiting is not always the most fun, but the psalmist David said, "I waited patiently for the LORD; He turned to me and heard my cry. He lifted me out of the slimy pit, out of the mud and mire; he set my feet on a rock and gave me a firm place to stand. He put a new song in my mouth, a hymn of praise to our God. Many will see and fear and put their trust in the LORD" (Ps. 40:1-3). Only He can put that new song in our heart. We must wait and then respond to His direction.

Avoid selfishness

Not long ago we were at a worship service and sitting in front of us was a young mother and two small children. As the service progressed, the worship leader was encouraging everyone to be more expressive. So the young mother and her children stepped away from their chairs to the large open area to give her and her children more room to express their worship. Suddenly an older woman, who we happened to know had recently lost her husband, came in with her head down, looking very lonely. She sat down in the middle chair, putting her purse on the chair beside her and books on the other chair, with no awareness that the chairs belonged to someone else. The little family stood for the rest of the service to avoid embarrassing the lady. They chose not to reclaim their chairs. The point is that this was not an act of willful rudeness. However, when we are so focused on our own centrality, we may conduct ourselves in such a way as to unknowingly offend those around us.

As we said earlier, it is hard to admit that some of our loneliness is because we are selfish and we look inward instead of outward. We need to look outward to the needs around us so that we can fill them. We need to rise above situations and reach out. It is not for us to be in the spotlight. God disappears when we insist on the spotlight. Then we are truly alone, so we need to focus on others and see how much it helps us with our loneliness as we watch it brighten their day.

Ask God to give you creative ways to reach out to others. God is in that business. He loves to help us bless others and in the process we are doubly blessed. Often we are His hands and His feet here on earth.

It is so easy to be full of ourselves in self-pity. We need to empty ourselves of pity and lean into Him. He is the ultimate fulfiller of a lonely heart. Remember, there is none sent away empty from Christ, except those who come to Him full of themselves. Loneliness often causes us to be full of ourselves. We should not view others through distorted lenses, looking for what we can get from another person rather than what we can give to them. Reaching out will help us have a better focus.

The story of Hagar in the Bible

In God's Word we find the story of Hagar (Gen. 16, 21:1-21), a story in which Abraham takes matters into his own hands. Because it seems his wife Sarai cannot bear a child, she urges Abraham to take Hagar, her maidservant, and Hagar becomes pregnant with a son. Then Sarai has a son Isaac, and Abraham sends Hagar away with her son Ishmael. Can you imagine the deep rejection and loneliness Hagar feels when Abraham sends her and her son away? But read on in the story and see her comfort and delight when God Himself speaks to her. He lets her know that He sees and understands her. He promises to be with her and love her. She is not alone after all. We take from this story how much God wants to be there for us. He will never leave or forsake us.

He never forsakes us

LeeAnn experienced this "never forsaking me" in a real way about a year after Willard died.

Her oldest son Mark and his wife Laurie were at a Youth With A Mission Discipleship Training School in New Zealand. It had been hard to let them go, but she knew Mark needed to get away after his dad died and seek the Lord as to what he was to do now with his life. So they went and she was happy that they were in a safe place and could spend time seeking God.

Then the test came. They called from New Zealand and said they felt God calling them to the Philippines for their outreach. LeeAnn was sure the connection was bad. The Philippines!? She had just heard that there was unrest there. "God, are you there?" she questioned, "Don't you remember I am here alone?" She was thinking about herself, she admits, not what was best for her son and his wife. She cried for several days. And she prayed, "Lord, help me find peace." She was thinking, if only Willard was here. Why did she have to face this all alone?

That weekend at a baby dedication the pastor said, "You know when our babies are small we say, 'Lord, wherever You want them to go, they are Yours. Use them. Timbuktu or wherever.' But when they grow up and God asks them to go to Timbuktu we say, 'No.'" It hit her how selfish she had been thinking only about herself and not the kids and what was best for them. She slumped in her seat. She prayed, "What was my concern? Willard and I had dedicated Mark to the Lord and had made that choice some twenty years before." A peace came over her and she felt God's wonderful presence as He wrapped His arms around her. Even in her selfishness He was there. He did not forsake her.

Our loneliness

When we find ourselves alone, either by death or divorce, we find a hole in our hearts that is deep. We feel so lonely and this can be a vulnerable time. Because of this loneliness it is easy to make a mistake. We must guard our heart and spend much time with the Lord if we want Him to help us.

In summary, it is important for us to work hard on our relationship with God. There and there alone is the true fulfillment we are all looking for whether we are married or single. We must spend time getting to know Him, reading His word and spending time in prayer. There are days when we do not feel like being in His Word, on those days we put on some good music and let the words of the song minister to our spirit.

Our lists

As we were trying to fill the void, we both made lists. Lists of what we wanted in a new mate if we were ever to marry again. We really wanted our first mates back. But that was not going to happen. So, as a safeguard against our vulnerability, we sat down and asked the Lord to help us make a list of qualities we would like in a new mate.

This may not be appropriate for everyone; we are all so different. But the reason we wanted to do this was to help us look at what was important to us – before the fact, not after the fact.

We could have each married someone else and it may have

worked. But we both feel that God had us for each other. And He helped bring us together.

Today (nineteen years later) as we write this, it all makes sense, but we remember those days of waiting for Him. Waiting is not fun. It is hard and it seems like such a waste of time. Then we are reminded that waiting for God is the most efficient use of time there is because we get in tune with Him during our waiting. All this waiting helps us adjust our inner senses and our hearts, and helps us align our will with His will. We can feel forgotten in this waiting time and feel that God is not there but in Isaiah 49:15-16 it says: "Can a mother forget the baby at her breast and have no compassion on the child she has borne? Though she may forget, I will not forget you! See, I have engraved you on the palms of my hands; your walls are ever before me." This verse in the Amplified Version reads: "I have indelibly imprinted (tattooed a picture of) you on the palm of each of my hands." Did you notice not just His hand but His hands!

Wow! How great is that? Trust Him; don't be impatient, just go with His timing.

Isaiah the prophet said:

> Do you not know? Have you not heard? The LORD is the everlasting God, the Creator of the ends of the earth. He will not grow tired or weary, and his understanding no one can fathom. He gives strength to the weary and increases the power of the weak. Even youths grow tired and weary, and young men stumble and fall; but those who hope in the LORD will renew their strength. They will soar on wings like eagles; they will run and not grow weary, they will walk and not be faint. (Isa. 40:28-31)

God is willing to help us fill that void. But we are so independent, often even afraid to trust Him. When we finally reach a place of surrender, He is there in an instant to carry us through with His wonderful love and grace that we so desperately need.

When we are going through a dark time it seems like this is the end; it certainly seemed like it to us when our mates died. Keep in mind that we have a very loving Father who will never leave us or desert us but will take every situation no matter how difficult and cause something good to come out of it. He has promised, "...all things God works for the good of those who love him..." (Rom. 8:28).

Chapter 4

WHY MARRY AGAIN?

L ET'S LOOK AT A REAL-LIFE situation of a man and woman who rushed into marriage without counting the costs and preparing for serious problems that might surface.

Ron's wife was killed in a car accident, leaving him to raise a teen-aged daughter alone. Two years later, mutual friends introduced him to Barb, a young widow with three kids, ages four to fifteen. Her husband had died of cancer the previous year. Within a few weeks, they were talking about getting married and did so six months later.

Everybody was delighted with the match. Neither one of them wanted to get into the "dating scene." Because each had enjoyed a good marriage with the deceased spouse, they assumed this second marriage would be a walk in the park. They knew and loved the Lord and had raised their children with biblical principles. What could go wrong?

Four years later, Barb filed for divorce, an admittedly desperate move aimed at holding her family together. Ron's daughter ran away and later accused Barb's son of molesting her.

Most of the issues between Ron and Barb were about the kids: how they did or didn't discipline them or how they disciplined them differently than their own.

Later the couple acknowledged how arrogant they had been. "We should have taken more time, given our children time to adjust," Barb said. "We should have gotten to know each other better before diving into marriage. The truth is, we were both so hungry for love, and we didn't want to wait."

The story we just recounted is one of many we have collected. This story shows that no matter how good your intentions are, if you don't take time to prepare properly and be very open and honest with each other, this could be your story in a few years. That is why we are writing this book – to encourage others to take time to be restored from hurts of their past and to take time to be open and honest as we go into remarriage.

Motives for remarriage

Now, let's look at some motives for remarriage. We encourage you to read over this list we have formulated and see which motive or motives fit you.

1. Loneliness – It is our conviction that God designed us to live together as husband and wife. Of course, there are exceptions and we certainly know a number of men and women who are whole, healthy people who remain single. But a greater number of us feel very incomplete and lonely when we have to spend our life alone. This was certainly the case in our lives. We felt we were not created to live alone and were not feeling fulfilled with the single lifestyle after being happily married for many years.

2. Financial insecurity – Many individuals realize how stressful it is to raise a family as a single mom or dad. This could be true for different personal reasons and

needs. Some decide to set up a household where two or more live together and have a much better lifestyle than they enjoyed before. The man often brings a different set of needs, hopes, and desires than the woman. But both may find that finances and the security of a home are high on their list. Just the hope of more income can bring the security that a single mom may be looking for.

3. Sexual desire – Here again God planted in all of us a desire for sexual expression. The joy of intimacy is one of the most wonderful aspects of a healthy marriage. When you have experienced this over a number of years, it is a great loss when it is not longer a part of your life. As Christians, we know this expression is to be inside of marriage, although some people choose not to marry and they fulfill this need with more than one person. We believe that this brings great harm to one's psyche and is a sin. It leads to even deeper loneliness and guilt.

4. The need to be cared for – We really do need to be loved and cared for by another human being. We feel this is especially true for women. Of course, men also feel there is nothing quite as wonderful as being cared for and loved by a woman. But the security that comes to a woman when truly loved and looked after is very high on her list of needs.

We know these are just a very few reasons why we marry again. Search your heart and see what the reasons are you want to remarry.

This is how it went for LeeAnn. It had been more than two

years since that fateful day when her husband of twenty-four years had gone to be with the Lord. Life seemed to go on. It seemed to go on whether she wanted it to or not. She filled her days with business. That got her through the days but then there were the nights. At first she did not want to go to bed, and then she did not want to get up.

Some days seemed to be a bit better than others. She was not sure what made the difference. Many things factored into that. Her friends were so good to her and always tried to include her, but she felt like a fifth wheel. Our world is so couple-oriented. Since remarrying she has tried her best to change that but it is not easy. One reason is that we have a hard time thinking single after thinking married all those years. It is not a battle of actions as much as a battle of emotions and thoughts.

About eighteen months after Willard's death, LeeAnn found herself in Kona, Hawaii, at a Discipleship Training School with Youth With A Mission. She highly recommends this to anyone, especially those who are at a crossroads in their lives. She found it to be such a safe place for singles. It was a place where life actually had some meaning. This was part of what God used to help restore her to love again. Her days in Hawaii were filled with life-changing times of teaching. She wishes she could say that being there took all the heartache away. It did not, but it gave new meaning to her life.

While there she felt that God was speaking to her, telling her to use what He had taught her and to teach others, especially the younger women, to love and cherish their husbands, to learn to respect them, and to be better wives. He also spoke to her about writing books and teaching on marriage.

This led her to a writing school in Texas about three months after she returned home. God miraculously allowed her book (*Loving Your Husband for Life*) to be published. But before that happened He did something even more wonderful in her life. He brought her a new husband. She told that story earlier in this book. He did not just drop him in her lap, but almost. She thought she had her life all planned, but neither she nor her new mate knew of "the Master's plan." But God did. They met and soon became the best of friends. The rest is history, great history.

How good God was to bring her not just an incredible man who had also lost his first wife, but who also had three great children. They were married in Hawaii. What a wonderful wedding it was, all six of their children joined them for the occasion.

As you read this you could be saying, beautiful wedding, wonderful guy, both have good families, what could go wrong? We could tell you that everything went very smoothly from this point on. But you know all of life is not that way. We're very pleased with the life we have had together and yes, many would assume that it's an excellent marriage and we lived happily ever after. This is true to some extent, but there are always those adjustments we need to make. The Lord has taught us and molded our character through these hard times.

Thinking back to life between the death of our mates and when we were married there were many days when we felt so lonely and discouraged. We both wondered if we would ever be happy again.

God often uses this dark time and difficult situations to help form our character. The building of our character may not happen when things are going smoothly and there are no problems. So when hard times come, lean into Him and trust Him as He does good work in you.

We have all heard that saying, " bloom where you are." We both realized that the "bloom" in the desert is even more beautiful. Any flower can bloom on the mountaintop where conditions are perfect. Blooming in the desert can be hard, but oh so rewarding.

Our Heavenly Father truly did bring us together and life has been wonderful. But, as we said, it has not been without its ups and downs. As we continue writing this book we want to explain some of the things we worked through. We did well on some but not all. Maybe as you read you can see some things that will help you in your remarriage. We also want to bring out some concepts we learned from other couples. These couples have remarried after losing their former mate to either death or divorce.

As we mentioned, one of the things we both did when we were single was to meditate before God and make a list of things that we wanted in a mate, should we ever marry again.

Duane's list was a bit longer than LeeAnn's but we both had some things on our lists that we were not sure God was going to bring us. But God had some great surprises for us.

Duane considers remarriage

Once Duane felt enough time and healing had taken place to move on in his life, he decided he was not designed to live alone. With this in mind, he had to give up any hope of getting Betty back while living here on earth. Therefore, he began to prepare his mind and heart for a second mate.

For Duane this required some very serious soul-searching. It became clear to him that he had to identify what he wanted in a mate. He was very aware of the fact that many second marriages fail because of lack of preparation and proper planning. The more he thought and prayed about it, the more obvious it became that if he wanted a good marriage he had to know what it takes to make a good marriage. He began to reflect on it.

Duane's first thoughts were that if he wanted a godly, mature wife, he needed to be sure that he was a godly, mature man to attract such a woman. He had been meditating daily on God's

Word for years so the best place to get his guidelines was from the Word of God.

It was difficult at first to know clearly what he wanted in a wife. But the more he thought and prayed, the clearer the picture became. This may not work for everyone but the discipline of sitting down and writing the character qualities desired in a new mate worked for him. If you choose to do this, he is sure your list will be different from his. It was very helpful to create an accurate picture of what he felt was most important to him in choosing a lifelong partner.

We do not want to go into great detail but God's principles are excellent guidelines to assist you in this process. Duane wanted to identify these character qualities, experiences, and basic beliefs before starting to court. For example, his spiritual life is most important to him. If he were to become one again with another woman he wanted to become one with a woman who had a strong and intimate relationship with God. Therefore, he placed on his list of values that she must be a mature woman of God who was a devoted Christian. Duane was unwilling to be one with an unbeliever or a shallow Christian.

As he worked through his lists of absolutes, important and desirable qualities, it greatly helped him to evaluate and pray about whom he would be interested in courting. In truth, it narrowed the field considerably, so much so that after reading over his list he questioned whether there was such a woman out there.

By principle, when you know clearly what you are looking for, it is much easier to cut to the chase and not be distracted by women who ultimately would not be a good fit. To Duane it was like shopping for a new car or house with no clue about what you really want. When you do this you may wind up buying the wrong car or house simply because there was a good salesperson. You bought because of your emotions or because you liked the looks but failed to look under the hood. You did not check out the basement for dry rot. Duane feels that he was richly rewarded for thinking it through before becoming emotionally involved.

Wrapped in our gift from God were all we had asked for and more. It is good to know what you might want so you are not so vulnerable in a time of loneliness that you make a horrible mistake. God knows even better than we do what we need and He loves to give us far more than we ask for.

When we met and determined we were right for each other, we wanted to get to know each other as quickly as possible. We looked for ways to get to know each other better. We did spend lots of time together, just talking and getting to hear each other's heart. LeeAnn had a manuscript of her first book (*Loving Your Husband for Life*) that was about to be published and Duane asked to read it to get better acquainted. In return, he gave her a few of the many personal journals he had been writing over the years. She took them home with her that weekend. She told him she could not put them down. By reading them, LeeAnn caught a glimpse of Duane's heart and decided, as she read (through tears), that the man who wrote these pages truly had a heart after God. She told Duane that she felt that any man who loved God so much would be a wonderful husband and they would have a great marriage. She also said that one of the main reasons she and God sat down to create her list was to protect her from making a mistake in choosing a mate who was not best for her.

Now, nineteen years later, that has proven to be true. We have had a great marriage – not without work, but good things do not come without work. Any marriage is work, but your marriage is worth all you can put into it. We cannot believe we are this happy again. But as you will see, happiness and contentment do not come without adjustments.

If you are not already remarried as you read this book but you are thinking about it, search your heart for the right motives and ask the Lord first to help you decide if you should remarry and then to help you in making the right choice in a new mate. If you are reading this and already remarried, make a conscious decision that whom you chose is definitely the best person for you and use the principles to make your marriage the best it can be.

Chapter 5

DEALING WITH
SEPARATION

Separation through death

IT HAS BEEN MORE THAN TWENTY YEARS since our first mates died. But even to this day, when we attend a wedding and hear the couple exchange their vows, when we hear the part where they say "till death do us part," our hearts are sad. Then we remind each other what it says in 1 Thessalonians 4:13: "[Do not] grieve, like the rest of men, who have no hope." In our minds death seems so final. But anyone who believes in Jesus knows we will meet our loved ones again. What a blessed hope. Next to seeing Jesus, never having to say good-bye will be one of the greatest blessings of heaven.

We had two very different experiences in losing our mates. Betty, Duane's wife, contracted cancer and lived for seven years. So they had time to process her illness, time to say good-bye. But for LeeAnn, Willard died so suddenly that they had no time for tender farewells.

We wondered, does anyone really process death even if there is time? Can one really say good-bye? There are different stories for each of us. Even in divorce some lose their spouse over a long period of time and for others, it happens quickly.

Each has its own set of difficult issues.

Separation through divorce

Not long ago we were having coffee with a single mom. She had heard we were writing a book on second marriages. She said, "I know the two of you had good first marriages and lost your mates through death, but do you have any idea what it is like to be separated from your mate through divorce or what my day looks like as a single mom?"

Then she shared from her heart the following — "My day usually starts very early in the morning, preparing breakfast and getting the children ready for school and day care.

"Then I rush off to do a full day's work at the office. Then comes picking the kids up, paying a hefty fee for the child care, and going off to the store to pick up that jug of milk that we always seem to need. Next I must fix dinner, while I play part-time referee and teacher's aide on homework.

"After I put the children to bed, there are bills to pay; clothes to wash, fold and put away; a house to clean; and then I fall into bed exhausted. It would be nice if I could go right to sleep but now comes the loneliness. There is no one to hold me, no one to share my hopes and dreams with, only ugly memories of abuse and misuse. I would love to put my ex-husband out of my life completely but he has the right to be with the children. I also realize that it is in the children's best interest not to dwell on his shortcomings. I must raise the children to love and respect their father, who hurt me so much. I often find my pillow wet with tears."

Our hearts go out to her. How she needs God's grace and our love.

We realize this is only one person's experience with separation by divorce. We know that some are not quite like this. We have some friends who divorced without being angry or bitter. They have encouraged the children to honor and respect the two different families and they go out of their way to make the children more comfortable with the fact that they are separated from their parent. We realize this is not the norm but it does happen occasionally. However, it seems divorce usually brings pain.

We have a friend who got a divorce, and is happily remarried. But he has said that if he had it to do it over, he would have worked harder at his first marriage. He would have tried harder to make it work, because of all the pain that the divorce has brought over the past twenty-two years.

Let's look at some of the issues separation brings.

Regrets

How do you deal with regrets? We hope you do not have a lot of regrets but everyone has some, whether you are separated by death or divorce.

We know we had a few regrets when we lost our mates. LeeAnn remembers one day feeling really bad as she thought back to the day Willard died. The day he died was a Saturday and she was busy cleaning the house. "If only I had taken more time to just sit with him that day," she thought. But how could she have known that this would be the last morning they would ever have together? She did get him different things, like making him some chicken soup, bringing him another pillow and blanket as he stretched out on the couch. They both thought he just had a case of the flu but soon learned how wrong they were.

LeeAnn was sharing this regret with her son one day and he lovingly looked at her and said, "Oh, Mom, all those times you were there for him count so much more."

Maybe you wish you had taken more time together or been a better mate. Not long ago a young widower told me with tears in his eyes, "Oh, how I wish I had known how to be a better husband in my first marriage." That same young man is now remarried and is a better husband to his second wife. So learn from your mistakes and grow from them; then they are not wasted.

Kari and John's story about regret

Kari and John were married for twenty years that fall. Christmas was just around the corner. Kari wondered if John would even think about a gift for her that Christmas. He sometimes did and other times just forgot. "Oh," she thought, "if only he knew what I would like." When he did get her something, he never seemed to get anything she enjoyed. Christmas came and John did get her a new blouse. But it surely was not what she would have picked out.

Now, nine months later, Kari is thinking back to that last Christmas they had together before the accident that took John's life. She remembered how John got that sad look in his eyes when she opened his gift and once again seemed disappointed rather than happy with the gift he had picked out.

How could she have known this would be John's last Christmas with her? She wished she had not been so picky about the things he chose for her. Why hadn't she just been grateful that he got her a present? It was no wonder John did not give her many gifts. As she related this story to us, tears filled her eyes. It saddened her heart when she realized the joy she missed and the joy she stole from him with her ungratefulness. How she wished she could roll back the clock and relive those moments when she had blown it.

Kari told us that whenever she has an opportunity, she shares with others not to be so negative. "Learn to show appreciation to those you love. So what if the gift is not just what you want? After all, the thought is what is really important."

If you're dealing with this kind of situation or one similar, don't beat yourself up. Like Kari, make the best of it and help others not to make the same mistake. In helping others, you will help yourself. Try to accept situations you cannot change. Choose to forgive yourself and go on.

Seeing things as they are

In our lives it seems that we see things best only in contrast. When we come out of the dark, light seems brighter and death suddenly helps us appreciate life. It makes life seem brighter. Loss makes us appreciate much more the love we had, flaws and all.

When we remarry it is easy to look back at our first marriage, especially if we had a good marriage, and think, "It was all so good, it is hard to remember the things that were not good." Our mind does this for us as a coping mechanism to help us through those first days and months, even years. But we must be real with ourselves, not dwelling on the flaws of our deceased mate, but acknowledging them. When we try to hold on too tightly to things that were actually not quite as we remember them, we may bring hurtful comparisons into our second marriage. So try to be honest with yourself and admit that your first mate was not perfect. It will help you be more accepting of your second mate.

Love goes on forever

We believe love goes on forever. LeeAnn has a Precious Moments collection and soon after Willard died, she received one sweet little statue that she still cherishes. On the bottom these words were written, "But Love Goes on Forever."

Allowing each other to continue to love our first mates is very important to us.

LeeAnn wondered how she could ever love anyone again because she knew she would always love Willard.

Then one day she was talking to a wise older gentleman and admitted to him that she did not know if she could ever remarry because she still loved Willard so much. When she expressed her doubts to him, he said, "LeeAnn, don't you have three sons?" She replied that she did. "Well," he said, "do you love only one of them?"

God has given us the capacity to love more than once. So hold on to the love of your first mate but do not feel guilty about the fact that you can love again. This is a gift from God.

What will happen in eternity?

Not long ago we were talking with a widow who had lost her husband about six months before. She asked us the same question that went through our minds when we first thought we might get married: "How have you worked out in your minds what will happen in heaven? If you remarry, whom will you spend eternity with?" We both smiled and recounted our story to her.

We told her that when we were first thinking about getting married, we said we wanted to spend eternity with our first mates. We both smile as we think back at what we believed. We thought we could get married and then bid each other farewell at the pearly gates and go spend eternity with our first mates. Now we have been married to each other for nineteen years and have grown in our love for each other. We told our friend who asked us that question that we trust God to work that out for us.

Speaking freely about our first mates

The issue of speaking freely about the other mate is one we all have to face. In our situation, death separated us from our first mates so it is easier to be free in speaking about them. With divorce, it would have been harder. But it is much healthier if you can feel free to speak openly about your former mate. We have experienced being around couples who will never allow their children to talk about their parent who died. How hurtful this is to the children. We feel they have gone through enough just losing their parent. We need to let them talk about that parent for their own health and well-being. We have found much comfort in sharing feelings with each other about our first mate.

In our marriage the freedom that we give each other is truly liberating for our children. There are pictures hanging in our home of our first mates. We encourage our adult children to talk about their deceased parent without any worry that they would be hurting or offending the stepparent. We likewise encourage the grandchildren to talk about their grandparent. We encourage you to talk to friends who knew your mate's former spouse. Find out what you can about them and pass these things on to your children or grandchildren. In our case, only a couple of grandchildren got to know their biological grandparent. Give your grandchildren the freedom to ask questions about their grandparent who is gone – in fact, encourage it.

How to deal with grief

Still another issue we deal with is the issue of how we grieve. We grieve differently and deal with issues differently. In Duane's case he has chosen not to visit Betty's grave because he knows she is not there. But LeeAnn has chosen to visit Willard's grave occasionally. LeeAnn also knows Willard is not there but she recalls one visit when her sons, their families, and she went to the graveside together. The boys brought their guitars. They spent time just singing and enjoying this sweet time of fellowship together. Neither way is the "right" way but we have given each other the freedom to do as each feels best.

Dealing with a deceased mate's personal possessions

Another thing you will need to consider is dealing with the personal possessions of your deceased spouse. In the grief process there is no right time for this to happen. In LeeAnn's case, she had given away or taken care of most of Willard's clothes and personal items before she and Duane ever met. But the time was shorter for the Rawlins family and circumstances were such that only Betty's personal things were taken care of. So when LeeAnn moved into their home, she had to go through many of Betty's things to make room for hers. This was a hard time for her and she shed many tears over the sadness of seeing the precious memories they'd had as a family. It did afford her to get to know her husband's first wife better. However, if she had to do it over again, she would not have put herself through that emotional pain.

We both understand the challenge of going through a mate's personal items. We soon realized that their new clothes, personal gifts, the things that were important to them when they were here on earth no longer had value to them, not even their wedding rings.

We are all different and timing may vary but there comes a point when items will need to be shared with others, given away or disposed of. We found it is sometimes helpful to have other family members, or a friend, to help you in this process.

Going through crisis in a new marriage

What do we do when we marry into a family that goes into crisis? Just a few years after we were married, Duane's oldest son Mark died of cancer, leaving four little children and a lovely wife.

It was hard for LeeAnn to know how to fit in; this was a new family. She wanted to be there for them but she felt she needed to give them space.

How well she remembers that day Mark died. The family decided to keep his body at home a little while before the funeral home was called. She can still see Mark's little boy, curled up on his daddy's chest where his heart was no longer beating. He cried himself to sleep there. She learned something that day. It is good for children to see death and healthy for them to grieve in their own way. In these times we need to do our best to fit in and love each other through them.

Helping others deal with the separation

These are just a few issues; we are sure there are others. The most important thing is to give each other the freedom to grieve in a way that helps the most. Be there for each other in love and understanding. Looking back, LeeAnn wishes she could have been there more for her sons as they worked through their loss, but it was all she could do to get herself through another day, she recalls. Somehow, by God's grace, they made it through those hard times.

But, if you find yourself in a place where there are children or young people going through grief over the loss of a parent, try to be there for them. Encourage them to talk to you about what they are going through. It is important that you just listen.

Often they do not need counsel, but a listening ear. Be sensitive to their hurting heart. We have experienced other situations in which children going through grief express their hurt in many different ways. Be aware of this and be sensitive to their needs in their healing. Ask God for wisdom and grace. He is there. All we need to do is ask.

Chapter 6

DANGER ZONE—
PROCEED WITH
CAUTION

IN THIS CHAPTER we want to discuss with you some areas that will help make your marriage successful.

We are aware that we will not cover all of the danger zones in marriage but these will give you something to think about. When you have finished this chapter, think of some areas that were danger zones in your first marriage, ones that we may have missed, and look for answers to those problems. List them and then take steps to put them to rest.

There are a couple of steps you can take to help you in this. First, pray and ask God to help you speak them out. After you have done this read the following passages, which talk about controlling our thought life: Philippians 4:6-9, Colossians 3:1, and Ephesians 4:23.

God's Word always brings insights and comfort.

Not being restored

This is what our book is about. We feel that you must be restored to love again. Keep in mind, when healing is complete you may still have the emotional scars, but not the open wounds that bring such pain into remarriage.

When we lose our mates to death or divorce, we are facing the death of our dreams, hopes, and aspirations. Give yourself time to grieve over these losses. Face them and deal with them but don't dwell on them.

Communication

We trust you are aware how important it is to have good communication in a healthy marriage. We tend to communicate differently. We have unique styles that often cause us to be misunderstood. Find out how your mate best communicates, and then be careful that you do not create roadblocks with your style of communicating. The secret of emotional oneness lies in the ability to communicate.

There are many factors that will improve your communications. One of these factors is timing. It's so important that you choose the right place and time to discuss certain subjects. If either mate is not in the mood to talk, it's not a good time to bring up difficult problems. You need to have privacy and a positive mental attitude if you're going to communicate in such a way as to resolve difficult situations in marriage or remarriage.

We have learned to communicate one way in our first marriage. Now we are in another marriage and things are quite different. It takes work to again learn how to communicate with a new mate, but the effort will pay off.

For us, LeeAnn was accustomed to Willard's quiet way; he was a very private person. Then, when she married Duane, she had to learn to adjust to someone who was a very outgoing and open person.

When LeeAnn counsels women, she often says, "I have been married to a very quiet, private person, and now I'm married to a very outgoing, open person, and neither is better. Each has his pluses and minuses. So no matter which type of communicator you are married to they are right for you. Learn how to communicate the way they communicate best.

LeeAnn remembers a funny story from when she was married to Willard. She was just a young bride. She has a problem with a heavy foot while driving a car and, sure enough, an officer was right there to pull her over. She was dreading the thought of telling Willard she had received a ticket. She got a great idea. Willard loved lemon pie. She would make a lemon pie and put her ticket under his piece of lemon pie. It worked! He laughed and enjoyed the lemon pie. Now, guess what – Duane hates lemon pie.

Comparison

Bob and Carol were married for thirty years. Bob died at fifty of a heart problem. They were so in love and they had a great marriage. Of course, it was not perfect but it was good.

About a year after Bob died Carol began to wonder if she should remarry. Some time passed and one night another single man from the church asked if she wanted to go to dinner. She decided she would go. During dinner all she could do was compare this gentleman with Bob. She was miserable and decided she would never find anyone like Bob. As time went on, another gentleman asked her out. The same thing happened every time she went out; no one measured up to Bob.

Carol became very discouraged. One night she was telling one of her sons about her frustration. What he said to his mom was really sweet. "Mom, do you really think Dad was as wonderful as you have made him?" Carol thought about what he asked. She knew her son loved his dad and knew he was a great guy. But she was also realistic enough to admit that he was not perfect. That day changed Carol's heart. Today she is happily remarried to a man who is not perfect and not like Bob, but someone she loves very much.

Comparing is one of the most damaging things that we can do to each other and to ourselves. It never helps to compare your second mate with your first. Often, after our mate has died, we remember the good things about our first mate and we forget about their frailties and faults. This creates an unrealistic and idealized picture that leads to an unfair comparison.

Two very negative things happen when we begin to make comparisons:

1. If we compare ourselves with others, we will always find that there's someone better. This leads to the feelings of insecurity and dissatisfaction with who we are.

2. When we compare ourselves with someone else and find we are better or think we are superior, pride will rear its ugly head.

Failure to understand uniqueness

The next quality that we would like to emphasize is the uniqueness of every individual. No one else on this planet has your fingerprints or your DNA. In recent years the whole DNA concept has been established where scientists can identify any person on earth by his or her DNA. There's no one else who has the same DNA as you. This means that we are unique and different from anyone else. The more we can understand that we are the only one of our kind, the happier we will be. Many of us initially love the uniqueness of the person we marry and then want to try to change the person.

Jim was very outgoing and always wanted to be the life of the party. Jane told us, "Before we were married, I loved how outgoing Jim was. I was quiet and reserved so his outgoingness was exciting to me. Then we were married and that same trait I loved so much often embarrassed me. He always seemed to have to be in the limelight. Year after year I criticized him for what I thought was showing off. Little by little he began to change. He was less confident and he became very quiet. At first I liked it because he was more like me but I soon began to realize that the fun and joy had gone out of our marriage. I found I really was not happy with the man he had become. Now we have a quiet, boring marriage with the sparkle gone."

Often the thing that made us fall in love becomes an irritant. We allow it to upset us rather then embracing each other's differences and enjoying life.

Harboring resentment

Resentment usually accompanies a tendency to be unforgiving and wanting to hold onto grudges. One can easily remember a hurt or wound that happened ten years before. The key to health and wholeness for this individual is to forget with one's mind and forgive with one's heart.

Rejection and criticism from someone you have loved can upset you only to the extent that you believe the words of the other person. If you let it linger it will destroy you, so don't hold on to the hurt.

Joe and Martha had been married for ten years. Each had been married before. Their daughter Jill was nine years old. Martha could not let go of the past. Numerous times when they would get caught up in an argument Martha would say, "You were not even there to take me to the hospital when Jill was born. You were out playing golf, like always, and our neighbor Fred had to take me to the hospital." Joe would once again try to explain that he was there for her birth. It was not a sign that he did not love her, he had no idea that her water would break and Jill would come two weeks early. But try as he would, she would not accept his asking for forgiveness for not being there when she needed him. Instead, she chose to nurse this grudge and hold it over his head.

We should learn from our past and not live in our past. Neither should we worry about our future, the key is to live in the present and learn from the past.

Being superficial

A superficial person is often shallow and unrealistic. This personality trait makes it easy to make friends quickly, but often out of sight is out of mind. Such a person quickly forgets offenses. In fact, he or she tends to forget almost everything and quickly moves on to the next exciting adventure. Often when a person is superficial, someone gets hurt. One moment he or she is loving, excited and appears to be your best friend, but in the next moment the person shows clearly that he or she is no longer interested in the circumstance or situation and is on to something new. This person needs to recognize his or her superficial nature and learn to be more genuine and be willing to go deeper. This person needs to learn to plant his or her feet on firmer ground and stay there.

Lifelong patterns

We have just mentioned a few of the differences in personalities but certainly we have not covered them all. As we look at traits in our own lives, we have found that we can change life habits but it is very difficult. We now have loved each other for the past nineteen years. During this time we have seen patterns in both our lives that have evolved from either childhood or early life patterns that have been extremely hard to set aside. We have consciously worked on these patterns to try to overcome them but it certainly isn't easy. We need to be careful that we do not allow personality traits to develop into bondage where we consistently act inappropriately because of previous hurts or wounds. One effective way to overcome this is to spend a great deal of time in the Word, allowing the Holy Spirit to transform, heal, and eliminate some of these deep wounds that we've never dealt with.

Adjustments

We would like to tell you that everything has gone very smoothly for us from the day we married. But you know all of life is not that way. We're very pleased with the life that we've lived together. Many would assume that it's an excellent marriage and that we are living happily ever after. This is true to some extent, but there are always adjustments that are necessary to make for a good marriage. We see how God used those dark times and difficult situations to help form our character. We have come to realize that this might not have happened if everything went smoothly. It often takes hard times for us to discover who we really are and what needs to change. We would encourage you to lean into Christ and trust Him. Allow Him to do a good work in you so that you will be restored to love again. Or, if you have re-married, look at the adjustments as character builders and make the ones you need to make.

Set aside time, at frequent intervals, for long talks about every aspect of your marriage. It is hard work but well worth the effort because you are working together at the most important investment – your relationship.

Chapter 7

SEX IN A SECOND MARRIAGE

A S WE SIT DOWN to write this chapter we smile. How can we ever do this justice? Good sex is so important in a marriage yet so hard to talk about, even to each other. It is such a wonderful gift from God. This gift the world has so misused, making something God created for our enjoyment within marriage into much hurt and misuse. Often, when we are counseling someone who is about to be married for the second time, we talk for a while about different issues and then invariably, the gal we are talking to looks away or turns a bit red as she says, "How in the entire world can you ever be intimate with another guy and have it be wonderful?" We always smile and say if we could explain it we would, but to us it is only a gift from God. This is especially true if your mate has died and you still love him or her. Somehow that love never dies. But God, through a miracle, makes us able to again enjoy intimacy with our second mate. And the only explanation we have is "only by a miracle can this happen."

God's wedding present

We believe when a couple gets married God gives them His own special wedding present designed for them to give them the greatest of pleasure. This gift should contribute to the oneness that also helps alleviate our loneliness. This gift is sexual intercourse.

Truly this is a mysterious union. God instructed us to fuse our bodies, and He promised that in so doing we would become one flesh. Becoming one flesh is something our minds cannot comprehend. But there is just no substitute for being one. Only God could create such a wonderful experience.

This miracle, especially in a second marriage, may not take place right away and will not always be painless and easy. Being kind and loving to each other is the key. Remember it is not about you but about each other. Women, especially, may take longer to adjust. Guys, give your new wife plenty of time and be understanding. You will be surprised how far understanding goes. Sometimes this miracle of complete oneness may take time and it may go more slowly than you hoped. But your patience and love will go very far with your new wife.

As we reread the above paragraph, we recognize that, for some, the sexual experience was not good in the first marriage. This could be true for someone divorced or widowed. So if the sexual life in the first marriage was not positive how does one enter into a second marriage with a healthy perspective of sex in marriage? Contemplating this matter we thought of a scripture, found in 2 Corinthians 1:4: "who comforts us in all our troubles, so that we can comfort those in any trouble with the comfort we ourselves have received from God." Perhaps God allows us to go through hard things so we can learn and then help others.

How does one explain this oneness? It is all at once both extremely wonderful and unfathomable. We believe that experiencing this oneness is the longing of every person who is willing to risk the emotional vulnerability of a second marriage. It truly is a miracle and a mystery that God can take two broken vessels and forge them into something new and beautiful. It is a feeling that is so wonderful to experience, yet so hard to explain.

Because we have already become one flesh with our first mates it can be so challenging in a second marriage to unite with someone else and become one. However, hard as it may be, it's not impossible. We smiled when we realized we were each marrying half of a person when we remarried after losing our mates to death. Our other halves were in heaven. Now we smile as we realize that we are whole again because we are one. Only God can cause this wonderful oneness to happen. This oneness happens when a husband and wife are intimate.

Being intimate is an issue that most couples do not like to discuss with others because it is so personal. But this area is such an important aspect of both first and second marriages.

It has been said, "When sex is right, everything is right." This may be a strong statement but surely not far from the truth. That is why God speaks about this wonderful union in 1 Corinthians 7:3-4. "The husband should fulfill his marital duty to his wife, and likewise the wife to her husband. The wife's body does not belong to her alone but also to her husband. In the same way, the husband's body does not belong to him alone but also to his wife."

The Bible calls sex "a mystery" by which two people, a man and a woman, become one. "After all, no one ever hated his own body, but he feeds and cares for it, just as Christ does the church— for we are members of his body. 'For this reason a man will leave his father and mother and be united to his wife, and the two will become one flesh.' This is a profound mystery—but I am talking about Christ and the church. However, each one of you also must love his wife as he loves himself, and the wife must respect her husband" (Eph. 5:29-33).

This Biblical description of "the mystery" gives a good guideline to follow in our marriage and gives a healthy picture of what a good marriage is, whether it is a first or second marriage. This "oneness" comes through our physical intimacy, an intimacy that communicates to both partners that they are loved. This "oneness" is even more of a miracle when we consider how different men and women are.

Differences in men and women

God has made men and women so very different. A book we have found helpful in this area of the differences between men and women is John Gray's book *Men are from Mars, Women are from Venus: The Classic Guide to Understanding the Opposite Sex.*

How each of us views sex in our new mate may be very different as well. Even in writing this book we see this chapter on sex much differently. Try hard to be open and respectful as you discuss how you might help each other with this most delicate problem. It seems that problems come when supposedly mature couples don't talk openly about sex or about their desires or what they enjoy.

One of the greatest communication breakdowns in the husband and wife relationship is in this area of sexual relationship. This is such a tender issue it is usually difficult to be open and vulnerable to each other. Because this is such a sensitive subject, often we inflict misunderstandings and hurts on each other. When there is a misunderstanding, if the wife gives in without resolving the conflict she feels resentful and if she backs off he feels hurt. Over the years we have observed that if one of the mates "stuffs" feelings and never shares, he or she ends up with all kinds of health issues. In some cases, not dealing with negative emotions can even lead to an early death. Try hard to be open and communicative with each other. Work hard at not hurting each other.

Two basic rules

We have come to believe that couples have a much better chance of finding a love that will last a lifetime by applying these two basic rules:

1. Avoid hurting each other
2. Work at meeting the emotional needs of each other.

You may be thinking that those are both great statements but you're wondering, "How do we avoid hurting each other, and how do we meet each other's emotional needs?" These are vital questions.

Let's look at the first "rule," avoid hurting each other. How do we hurt one another? It seems that one of the ways we hurt our mate the most is to speak negatively about him or her. This is especially true when it is done in front of friends or family As we said earlier it takes ten *atta boys!* to make up for one put down. Why do we put each other down? Is it to build ourselves up? Think about it – isn't it foolish to tear down the very people we choose as our mates? Try hard to look at the good and not focus on the negative. This principle also applies to our thought life even if we do not speak the words to our mate. Keep your thoughts about each other positive. We will see faults in one another, but the key is not to dwell on the faults. Give your mate and his or her faults to the Lord. He is much better at changing our mate than we are. Perhaps as we release our mates to the Lord we will be changed, too.

We have a simple analogy that illustrates this point so well. Take a quarter and think of the quarter as the fault. If you hold that quarter ever so close to your eye it is all you see, but it you hold it an arm's length you see a lot more and aren't so focused on the negative. You can see the good as well as the fault. It is all about perspective.

Sometimes we hurt because we have been hurt by our mate or by others. God says He will take care of our hurts but he requires that we give those hurts to Him and release forgiveness. He knows so much better how to deal with those who hurt us. Trust Him and don't take matters into your own hands; it only causes more pain. The cycle of hurting can be endless and is always destructive

We are sure there are many ways we hurt each other, sometimes on purpose and sometimes very innocently. Nevertheless, hurts hinder our relationship and often take so much time and work to get over. It is best to avoid, at all costs, those things that you know will hurt your mate. Try to learn to be quick to repent and quick to forgive.

Meeting each other's emotional needs

Now let's look at the issue of meeting each other's emotional needs. Wow, this is a big one. Each person is so different and our needs are so different. The first thing is to try to identify our mate's needs. What blesses our mate, what brings a smile to a tired face, what brings joy? Often we think we know what might bless someone and it is not a blessing at all; it does not meet their needs.

Try not to be too needy; appreciate each small need your mate meets, let your mate know when he or she meets a need. Here may be a good place to say a bit about expectations. Make your "need bank" small. If we don't expect, then every need that is met is a true gift. We tend to put too high an expectation on our mates. That is why we are hurt so often, because we have unmet expectations that we foolishly put on each other.

Do you know what love really is? Let's look at what the Bible says in 1 Corinthians 13 about the true meaning of love. *The Message* says this:

> *Love never gives up.*
> *Love cares more for others than for self.*
> *Love doesn't want what it doesn't have.*
> *Love doesn't strut.*
> *Doesn't have a swelled head.*
> *Doesn't force itself on others.*
> *Isn't always "me first."*
> *Doesn't fly off the handle.*
> *Doesn't keep score of the sins of others.*
> *Doesn't revel when others grovel.*
> *Takes pleasure in the flowering of the truth.*
> *Puts up with anything.*
> *Trusts God always.*
> *Always looks for the best.*
> *Never looks back, but keeps going to the end.*

As we reread this passage, we admit that it is so easy to read this and decide in our heart to follow this, but we know that walking it out is so much harder. But with God's help we can truly live much closer to the reality of what we just read. Ask Him. He is so willing to help us. He says that we have not because we do not ask (James 4: 23).

Love is a wonderful gift we give each other. It is in this gift of love that our God has given us. Part of this wonderful love that God has given us is the wedding present, sexual intercourse, given to us so that we can come together and bring new life. This is not necessarily to create a baby, but rather a form of spiritual oneness. This oneness can be a deepening of our understanding of each other and can bring healing of some hurts that may have been inflicted on us from the past.

To forgive or not forgive

It is so important that we forgive our first mate and not bring old hurts from our first marriage into the second marriage. It is time to let them go if you haven't already. We know that forgiveness costs, but don't forget that the price tag of resentment demands continual payments. Don't bring these payments into your second marriage. To relinquish resentment, first identify it, then forgive yourself, then forgive your former mate for what he or she did to you.

Forgive. Decide to do it today if you have not. A few steps in forgiving are:

1. Find out the source of the hurt and deal with it

2. Give the pain and hurt to the Lord. We have a saying, "What you don't reveal, God does not heal."

3. Ask God to give you grace to forgive and move on.

If you hold resentment toward your former mate it will keep you living in the past. Retired U.S. Senate chaplain and author Lloyd Ogilvie says, "The sure sign that we have an authentic relationship with God is that we believe more in the future than in the past. The past can be neither a source of confidence nor a condemnation. God graciously divided our life into days and years so that we could let go of yesterdays and anticipate our tomorrows. For the past mistakes, He offers forgiveness and an ability to forget. For our tomorrows, He gives us the gift of expectation and excitement."[2]

Un-forgiveness hinders this miracle of oneness, so taking care of past hurts is extremely important. A good rule is to deal with your hurts as they occur. Never let the sun go down on your wrath. Forgiveness occurs when the person becomes more important than the problem. Forgiveness is hard, especially the forgetting part. In fact, God forgives and forgets but we are not God; we can and must forgive but can't always forget.

Sometimes the hurt comes back to your memory when you have already forgiven. Speak out forgiveness again. Cry out to God for His grace. He will meet you in your hour of need. Keep doing this each time the temptation to resent comes back, and over time the memory will have less and less impact on your emotions, and your feelings will catch up with the choice already made to forgive. The oil of forgiveness will continue to soften that sore till it heals and goes away. You can get to the point where you may remember what happened, but there is no longer the sting, the pain that was once attached to the thought. This is the miracle of forgiveness. This process may take longer, depending on the depth of the pain. Remember that the healing process in your heart may happen over a period of time.

One wonderful example of forgiveness that we read in the Bible is the book of Hosea. The story of the harlot Gomer and her husband Hosea, who found it in his heart to forgive her over and over. It is a wonderful story of love and forgiveness. Author Francine Rivers' wonderful novel *Redeeming Love* puts this story into the 1850's Gold Rush era in California. You may want to get a copy of it and read it if you are having problems forgiving.

We personally know a wonderful story of forgiveness that happened in our lifetime.

This young couple started out, as most couples do, madly in

love and ready to have a lifetime of happiness together. But down the road they drifted apart, she becoming the best mom ever and he finding success in the line of work he had chosen for his life. Their drifting apart did not happen overnight. It seems she was so wrapped up in the kids, she was just too tired and too busy to give her husband the attention he needed. She was not completely to blame, but he did not offer to help her and found more and more reasons to stay at work longer. They just drifted apart. It all happened so unexpectedly. He was at work one day and a young girl came into his office telling him how unhappy she was. He, too, was unhappy, so he listened. Soon she was in his office more frequently. He found himself starting to enjoy these times together. He would ask her out to lunch so they could talk more. You know the old story, one thing leads to another and before too long he found himself being unfaithful to his wife.

Of course, this did not bring happiness to either party involved. It only posed a dreadful question of how he was ever to tell his wife. He now realized what a fool he had been. He was caught is such an awful trap. As time went on, he became so miserable. One day he could stand it no longer. He went to his wife and told her the ugly truth.

This young wife made a choice that day. This was not an easy choice to make. But in the scope of things it surely was the wisest choice. She chose to forgive her husband that day. It was not something she took lightly, nor did he. It took many years of love and more loving for him to earn back the trust he once had. But if you were to talk to this young lady (now middle aged) she would tell you that forgiveness is surely the right choice – not the easiest, but surely the best.

In our lifetime we have had several friends who have chosen to forgive when one or the other has been unfaithful. In every situation the one who chose to forgive has been rewarded. Of course we cannot say how their lives would have played out had they chosen not to forgive but we can look at those who have not made this choice and see the ramifications of this un-forgiveness on their life. Often, marriages in which the choice was made not to forgive ended in divorce, which has brought suffering and pain to them and to their children, not to mention the ugliness that sets in when we are unforgiving. Forgiving is not easy – but it is truly the wisest choice.

Dealing with pornography issues

Another issue that some couples have to deal with, and have a hard time communicating with their spouse about, is pornography. Read on as a friend Darla shares her struggle with this issue and how she dealt with it. She writes:

"This issue may be a sensitive one, but I want to share it because I believe it could help others who may be in a similar bondage. Before I became a Christian, I'd gotten involved in pornography. Not looking at pictures or watching videos, but reading titillating books filled with sexual fantasies.

"Within a few weeks of becoming a Christian, I was convicted by God and I burned all the books. But the images stayed in my brain. After we were married, those fantasies played in my mind while we were making love. I knew it was wrong and I needed to get them out of my head, but how?

"I prayed and asked God for a strategy. I believe He led me not to share this battle with my husband yet, but to take certain steps. The first was the hardest. I gave up my right to ever enjoy sex again. I prayed, 'Lord, I want you to purify this area – even if it means I never have another orgasm in my life.' I meant it. The Lord would know if I was faking.

"The second step was doing battle mentally. I felt that God

prompted me to visually imagine the loving things my husband was doing to me as we made love and to superimpose those new images over the old fantasies plaguing my mind. It worked! Not the first time, of course. In fact, it took nearly six months of battling mentally until the new loving images of my husband automatically came to mind.

"The enemy assaulted me during that time, bringing all kinds of perverted thoughts to me. But with God's help, I kept my eyes on Him (mentally) and my thoughts on my husband. This was quite a balancing act! Remember my husband was making love to me (my body) while I was fighting the enemy (my mind). Eventually the Lord released me to share with my second husband, because the last step was crucial and we needed to do it together.

"If a wrong image popped into my mind, I would begin praying in the Spirit (in my prayer language) and my husband would join me. He would know by that clue that I was being tempted and by praying with me, he strengthened our battle against the enemy.

The freedom from this bondage was *and is* an incredible miracle in my life."

Pornography certainly can be a problem when you remarry. No matter how well you get to know your future mate, this secret may not be revealed until after the wedding day. With easy Internet access, this may be the biggest "secret sin" in the church today.

Ephesians 4:29-32 says, "Do not let any unwholesome talk come out of your mouths, but only what is helpful for building others up according to their needs, that it may benefit those who listen. And do not grieve the Holy Spirit of God, with whom you were sealed for the day of redemption. Get rid of all bitterness, rage and anger, brawling and slander, along with every form of malice. Be kind and compassionate to one another, forgiving each other, just as in Christ God forgave you."

Healing from premarital sex

The following story, which was told to us, is a beautiful picture of forgiveness to each other and from God. He wants us to forgive and He is ready and willing to forgive us. Be encouraged as you read this story as told to us.

"We fell into a sexual relationship right away. We didn't know the Lord then, and it's the way of the world. But in God's timing, just six weeks later, we accepted Jesus into our hearts.

"Immediately the Holy Spirit began to convict us of our sin. We planned to be married so we went to the priest for counsel. He gave us permission!! He told us the Bible forbids fornication, but that didn't apply to us since we planned to get married. Right there in his office, we took a deep breath and said we believed God was calling us to obedience and that He had a higher purpose.

"We chose to listen to God, not man, and committed ourselves to stop having sex until we were married ten months later. God taught us during that time that we had both misused our sexuality in the past and He wanted to purify us. We knew nothing about boundaries and had some close calls early on. There were times we were half undressed and managed to get on our knees. God always gave one of us the strength to resist. In time, we learned new boundaries and were able (by His grace) to remain chaste.

"Would it surprise you to hear we were like virgins on our wedding night? We had to learn everything all over again! What a wonderful wedding gift from the Lord! In His mercy and grace, He gave us such a sweet union plus supernatural understanding of the power that unity brings to marriage. We guard that carefully.

"I believe one reason infidelity has never been a problem for us, in addition to our commitment to the Lord, is that we were faithful to each other in those months before marriage. Coming out of a previously promiscuous lifestyle, that is an important distinction.

"When I first became a believer I heard that the Holy Spirit has two jobs to do: To get you out of the world and then, to get the world out of you! To the extent you were 'in the world,' this takes more time for some than others. For me, it took a long time!"

Communication and sex

We must learn to be open with our thoughts and feelings. God wants us to openly communicate freely in every area of our relationship and especially in this area of sex. It is hard for me to stress strongly enough the importance of good communication. Many problems, perhaps even 50 percent of all sexual problems, could be solved by open and honest communication. Find a good Christian counselor to help you understand each other better or read a good book on this subject.

A couple of books we recommend are Jerry Jenkins' book *Loving Your Marriage Enough to Protect It* and Ken Near's book *Understanding the Mind of a Woman*.

Communication is so important in life and especially in our love life. Communicate with each other about what ministers to you, what you enjoy, then do those things.

Building intimacy

We should look at several things that lead to wonderful intimacy, both in a first and second marriage. Atmosphere, moods, and timing all have so much to do with a wonderful time of intimacy. Women especially love to be touched, touched in very special ways. Be careful to take care of yourself by bathing, watching your weight, making yourself more pleasurable to be with. Men seem to be affected by how we look and smell. Sex for a woman seems to be more in her head. She is greatly affected by how she is touched, what is said, how tender her lover is with her. She loves it when her man sets the mood by lighting candles, turning on romantic music, or doing whatever he knows will bring enjoyment to her.

It is important to get away together. If your budget does not allow large expenditures, do things that do not cost much, things like a picnic or a dinner out (even if it has to be fast food). Take a drive somewhere that you both enjoy. You could read the Song of Solomon together. We enjoy reading it from the Living Bible, sitting together by a nice fire.

Be creative. Ask God to help you to be creative. It is important to remember that it is not just about me, it is about us. Someone said "Every marriage needs to be picked up and hugged and given personal attention" (source unknown). This is even more important in second marriages.

Differing needs as we age

In a second marriage we are often older, and along with being older may come several things that are different than when we were young. The desire for the sexual act may not be as great as we grow older but the need for intimacy is always there. Work this out between you. It would be best to sit down and talk this through, possibly with a counselor before you remarry. Try to understand each other's needs. Be loving and tender toward each other. To us, there is just a certain beauty about an older couple deeply in love. By way of contrast, one of our pet peeves is seeing an older couple bicker at each other. Don't fall into that trap of constantly disagreeing and making negative comments toward one another. This trap is so easy to fall into. Keep your love fresh and creative.

Since we may be older when we are in a second marriage, we hope we are wiser. This wisdom and experience should help in building a happy sex life in a second marriage.

We wish we could say that sex in a second marriage is always easier but it is not; it is often harder. In your first marriage you did not have to share your partner with anyone, nor did your partner have to share you with anyone. But in a second marriage if one or both of you have children, you may end up with a lot less time together than you would like. Not only is time a problem, it is also an energy problem. Having children and the responsibilities that go along with them requires more energy. Learn early on to set aside time for each other; this is so important. This is a major problem in many second marriages. The following are some stories from other couples who have faced this problem of adjusting to a new marriage and a family all at once, and have learned to deal with the changes well.

Take time to plan

Phil and Janet went into their second marriage with two children each. Phil's were fourteen and twelve; Janet's were ten and eight.

Before they were married they sat down and talked through

their situation. They found that when they were single parents all of their time and energy was consumed in just providing for their families.

As they talked they decided to sell both their homes and purchase a new slightly larger home for their blended family.

Then Janet and Phil were married. They did sell their homes and from the sale of their homes they were able to make a good down payment on their new home and pay off the debts they had. They were even able to set aside a small amount to use for family fun. Both Janet and Phil had learned that that there were a lot of things that they could do as a family that were inexpensive and still fun. Their marriage was not without its share of problems but the planning ahead that they had done truly helped make their marriage work well. Having this huge problem solved ahead of time, rather than after the fact, greatly enhanced their intimacy with each other and got them off to a good start.

Get resolution ahead of time if possible

Joe and Betty, who also had been married before, had made several mistakes when they met. Like Phil and Janet, they had several children between them. They were both so lonely and so anxious to fill that hole in their hearts. Nevertheless, wisdom would say that taking the time to at least define some of the issues and seek some resolution before getting married could save a lot of heartache further down the line.

Often loneliness can hinder you from thinking clearly, as was the case with this couple. They very quickly got married, thinking they would just work out the problems as they came. This is not a good idea because there will be plenty of issues or problems that will come after you get married. Not only is it good to work on these issues before you decide to marry, but it is also is good to see how you can work together solving issues and problems together.

Needless to say, Joe and Betty found the problems were greater then they thought. Their sexual relationship was almost non-existent due to all their problems. Soon they found themselves involved in a second breakup.

As we look at these stories we find it is so important to take time together and work out all that you can in advance of marriage. Then keep in mind that the first year together is so important to build and bond your relationship. The reason it is harder is because with less time available, it may take longer and be more challenging. Give God, with the Holy Spirit, time to work on you, inside your hearts. He specializes in changing hearts.

In a second marriage, the chance of happiness and a fulfilled sex life may be less likely, but surprisingly these same things may also enhance your marriage. A good second marriage may mean more to those who have experienced pain in a difficult first marriage. We hope we learn from our failures in our first marriage, especially when we brought unrealistic expectations into the marriage.

In a second marriage, as in any marriage, learn what blesses your mate. Don't assume that you know, because you can be so wrong. We found that we had to relearn what pleased each other in our second marriage just as we had in our first marriage. We are all very different and what pleases one may not please another. So work at finding what pleases your mate. You have spent years learning to know what made your first mate happy. It will take time so don't expect to learn what pleases your second mate overnight. Take time, and enjoy the process.

Logistical adjustments

We found another issue that has been a problem, especially for many women. This issue is that of purchasing a new bed. This may not seem as important to men, but it is often an issue for women. If at all possible, avoid using either of your former beds. If you can't afford to buy a new bed, at least go out and buy new sheets and bed covers.

That first year in a new marriage can be difficult with the numerous adjustments, so it is very important to be sensitive to one another's needs and preferences. Be gentle with each other on sad days or when your mate is working through a memory. It's difficult so be sensitive to each other, especially in that first year. We do not know what it is like if you find yourself in a second marriage in bed with your new mate following a divorce. But we do know when you lose your first lover by death, all we can say is that God does perform miracles in this, a hard adjustment. Don't compare in any area, but especially in the area of sex. Just trust Him in this.

In spite of all the adjustments and problems a second marriage brings you, you can find fulfillment and happiness. This takes time and work; you must plan together, pray together, and play together. Always be persistent when you work through problems. Remember that it can work and sex in a second marriage can be wonderful and fulfilling. It is your choice; you must simply choose to make it work. Don't despise this wonderful gift God has given you, but love and cherish it. It must be your heart's purpose that your sex life in your second marriage will be good.

Attitudes

As we think about sex in a second marriage, so much depends on our attitude, as does so much of life. We would like to conclude this chapter with a well-known quote on attitude by Charles Swindoll:

> The longer I live, the more I realize the impact of attitude on life. Attitude, to me, is more important than facts. It is more important than the past, than education, than money, than circumstances, than failures, than successes, than what other people think or say or do. It is more important than appearance, giftedness or skill. It will make or break a company...a church...a home. The remarkable thing is we have a choice every day regarding the attitude we will embrace for that day. We cannot change our past. We cannot change the fact that people will act in certain way. We cannot change the inevitable. The only thing we can do is play on the one string we have, and that is our attitude. I am convinced that life is 10 percent what happens and 90 percent how I react to it. And so it is with you... we are in charge of our attitudes.

Chapter 8
BLENDED FAMILIES

If it is possible, as far as it depends on you, live at peace with everyone.
—Romans 12:18

Falling in love

WHEN WE, AS DIVORCED or widowed people, begin a relationship, the emotional rush of falling in love can easily cloud our judgment, especially in relationships where children are a factor. Objectivity seems to vanish when we as parents try to sell our kids on the idea of a potential stepparent entering their world. If the children have adjusted to the idea that we are dating, we might quickly conclude that they will also accept our new love as a parent. Think again. Children have to learn to love and trust a new parent figure and that will take months if not years.

We've often heard love-struck couples say, "How hard can it be to blend our families? We love each other so much. Surely our love will carry us through the rough spots."

These are the ones who typically rush to get married and then find themselves in a mess.

Love does cover lots of problems, but it takes hard work to blend two families. In the first year of a new relationship, we have to continually work at getting to know each other's children, earning their trust and respect, and building bridges of communication and friendship.

Blended

The term blend means "to mix smoothly and inseparably." However, on a kitchen blender the word "grate" comes before "blend," and that's usually what happens first when two families come together. This grating takes place as kids test the boundaries of their new family environment. Stepparents who don't have a plan for how to handle this series of tests and the many deeply emotional issues that will come up will surely be *grated* themselves. These issues include disciplining each other's children, handling decisions that affect the whole family, the special problem of being a part-time parent (in joint custody situations), family traditions and holidays, the possibilities of moving to a new home or church, and the list goes on.

The children

Whatever anxiety you may be feeling about impending change is likely to be multiplied in your children. Consider what it is like for them. They have lost one parent to death or divorce. Now their remaining parent (you) is changing dramatically because of your need to adjust to your new spouse. They see you struggling to divide your time between them and your new mate. They don't yet know the rules or how this new stepparent will treat them or you. No wonder many children feel abandoned or fearful about this process.

In writing this we do not pretend to have all the answers, but we have gleaned much from our experience and that of other families who have also gone down this road. In learning from their successes and failures, we have hope that many more second-marriage families can get beyond the grating stage and start blending. God has given us the tools to help us in the process, but we have to be willing to change. Most of those we interviewed said that their second marriages required far more adjustments than they had to make in their first marriages. They also required a deeper dependence on God to change those areas in others (particularly our children) that we were powerless to change ourselves. By applying His wisdom and drawing on His power, there is great hope that many more second marriage families can live together in an atmosphere of love, mutual respect and consideration.

Where will we live, your house or mine?

This question of where to live has more potential for problems than any other single issue. A home is filled with memories, both happy and sad, and changing simple things like the pictures on the wall can have the effect of ripping out a piece of your heart. This two-edged sword can do damage on both sides – for the new family moving in and bringing all their favorite "stuff" (which may not blend at all in the new home) and for the original family who has to make room in their home (and daily physical space) for the new people and their things. Is it any wonder that children who've grown up in the home may feel like their new stepsiblings are intruders?

We know a widower with three daughters who moved from Boston to Sacramento to marry a divorcee with three children, ages nine to fourteen. His girls were eager to move to California, which made that decision an easy one. They had the means to buy another home, but they all agreed that the smoothest transition would come from the man and his daughters moving into the family's large house. It seemed like sound logic: 1) Three kids wouldn't have the "moving" adjustment to make and could go on with their lives in the same schools, same neighborhood, same friends; 2) The newlyweds wouldn't have the added stress of finding or building a new house, packing and moving; and 3) There was plenty of room for everyone to have their own space, including a blending of their cats and dogs.

Big mistake! This couple is divorced today after six years of continual grating between the two sets of children and between children and stepparents. In retrospect, this couple now wishes they had started fresh in a new home. In their reasoning, they neglected to weigh the unseen emotional consequences of their decision. When heated arguments arose, the woman or her children would sometimes shout, "Get out of my house!" The man and his daughters never felt like it was truly *their* home.

In LeeAnn and Duane's situation, Duane offered to build a new home when he proposed to LeeAnn. In her desire to be financially prudent, she deferred, suggesting instead, "Let's just live in your house, and I will remodel and redecorate." Later she realized that it was not the best idea. She knew it could not have been easy for the Rawlins kids to see her change their mother's house. And for LeeAnn's sons, they told her it never seemed like it was their home. LeeAnn believes it is best to find a home that is different than either spouse's former home. LeeAnn and Duane finally did that, and it was one of the best decisions of their marriage.

Our research shows that this is one of the most emotionally volatile issues in a second marriage. Little changes you make can have a big emotional impact on your spouse or his or her kids. For example, as the new wife living in the home of her predecessor, perhaps you gave away or threw out a few boxes of odds and ends. The next time his kids come for dinner, they ask where certain salt and pepper shakers are, the pair their Mom always had on the table. You may be mortified but it's too late.

After we married, we moved into Duane's house where Lee-Ann found many reminders of his first wife Betty. Through little notes and personal items she found, she got to know and love this exceptional woman. But she often found herself in tears. They were not tears of jealousy, but genuine sadness that she was no longer there to enjoy her wonderful family. They obviously were so close, and at times she felt like an intruder in her new home. Each instance was such a sad reminder that she was the "step-mom." How would she ever be able to fill the void left in the hearts of Betty's children and grandchildren?

She realized now that she might have avoided some sad days if she had allowed Duane to build a new home for her.

When we decided to build a new home *together* and deal once and for all with all the memorabilia, photo albums, etc. from our past marriages, our lives became so much easier. It was like having a clean start. Of course there are still things in our home from our past marriages, but they bring us comfort rather than sadness now that we are further down the road and the pain is not so fresh.

"If you must move into an existing home, where your husband and his children live, your concern should be that everyone's space is respected," writes Dr. Beth E. Brown, in her book *When You're Mom No. 2.* "Space represents belonging. The house belongs to the whole family, but everyone has his or her own individual space…If Mom No. 2 brings her own children to the second marriage, space conflicts can be monumental. If possible, she should keep children in their own rooms and avoid doubling up. The children's need for privacy may never be greater than in the first few years of stepfamily life."[3]

Sharing custody

One of the most difficult "blending" challenges in a second marriage is when there has been a bitter divorce and parents share custody. In his book *Living Beyond Divorce*, author Jim Smoke sees advantages to both weekly visitations and more extended annual visits. "Living away can deliver one from being an entertainer parent and constant combatant in the post-divorce wars that often set a record for longevity. Fifty-two Saturdays a year might better fit two summer months of concentrated time with a parent living out of state. The struggle with this is that a distant parent misses out on the 'dailies' of their child's life: homework, ball games, birthdays, the flu, boyfriends, and girlfriends, to name a few."[4]

"Visiting stepchildren create special challenges," says author Charles Cerling. "They bring far more stress into your life than full-time stepchildren ... While you might not be close, you can work out a functional relationship."[5]

One way to build a foundation for a functional family relationship is to create a permanent space for your part-time children. If you don't, they will never feel as if they belong there. "Permanence is the key issue. You let them know that they are a permanent part of your life by providing them a place of their own in your home ... [assuring them] you will be there for them as long as they need you," says Brown.[6]

Starting points on the path to acceptance

Accept one another, then, just as Christ accepted you. —*Romans 15:7*

The great longing of every stepparent and every stepchild is for acceptance. We want our spouse's children to accept us and respect us in our new parental role, but getting to that point may be a long and bumpy road.

From the moment you move in, everything you say and do will be noticed and compared to the way things were before. In some cases this will be a positive thing, but more typically children notice differences that they perceive as negative. You can never fully replace your stepchildren's missing parent so don't try to do everything the way he or she did. Establish your own parental identity that reflects your personality and the values you share with your spouse. Pray together for special insight into each child's emotional needs, and take time to listen for keys to establishing good communication. One early issue is how you will address one another.

When LeeAnn first met Duane's daughter Mindy, she said to LeeAnn, "Oh, you are so perfect for my dad, but what am I going to call you?" She thought a bit and then said "LA – that is what I am going to call you." So now she is LA to his children and her children call Duane "D." It has worked well for them; it is an endearment but does not replace their "Mom" or "Dad." Don't ever force your spouse's children to call you Mom or Dad. Typically the younger ones are more likely to accept you in that role. Older kids may never call you Mom or Dad, and that's okay. Find a name that's acceptable to both and respectful of your new role in their life. We found that sometimes our children call us Mom or Dad, especially when they are introducing us. It is just easier then trying to explain. The main point here is to allow your children to have the freedom to address the new parent in the way that is comfortable for them.

In his book The *Blended Family: A Guide for Stepparents,* Ralph Ranieri says that we too often come into a second marriage with unreasonable expectations. "Keep your expectations at a minimum. Start with respect. If your stepchild treats you with respect, then relax. Respect is fundamental. Once you have this, many other good things will flow into the relationship if you give yourself and your children time to make adjustments."[7]

The perceptive stepparent will recognize that to go deeper we need to discover the keys to each child's heart. Michelle Pearson, a mother of four and stepmother of three children, recommends that stepparents identify and speak to each child (and to their spouse) in their "love language," a communication tool promoted by author Gary Chapman in his book *The Five Love Languages*. These five include quality time together, words of affirmation, gifts, acts of service, and physical touch. Pearson says that communicating in one's love language is like making a deposit in an "emotional bank account."[8] A child's birth parent may have known this language intuitively, but stepparents usually learn as they go.

Another thing stepparents must learn soon is how to define the life issues about which they are willing to confront the kids. A friend who raised six children once said to us, "Don't major on the minors. Pick your battles. Be the grown-up. Use the hundred-year rule (Who's going to care in a hundred years?)."

When you do have to confront an issue with your new children, try to put your own feelings aside in the dialogue. Love and accept them even when they do not accept you. You cannot lose by loving. In the end love wins. In our culture we have come to expect quick solutions, but acceptance by stepchildren is rarely quick. Keep in mind that the children have experienced a devastating loss and are facing a new world full of uncertainties. So give yourself time to woo them, to win their trust and establish a relationship. Remember, they are the immature ones (at least that is how it would seem) so show them grace and patience.

A key part of this blending process is the recognition that you cannot do it alone. No one can. The issues involved are too big, too emotionally charged for you to overcome. That's why you need the Lord. Cry out to Him for wisdom and strength when you need it. Pray with your spouse daily about family issues. Seek the counsel and prayer support of godly friends. Don't let pride keep you from reaching out for help from your pastor or your Christian friends. More and more churches are recognizing that they need to rally around stepparents in their congregations.

In a *Breakpoint* column on the *Breakpoint* Web site, ministry leader Charles Colson writes:

> Pastor Dick Dunn of Roswell, Georgia, didn't pay much attention when a couple in his church asked for help in dealing with hostile stepchildren. After all, the husband and wife were strong Christians. "Surely," he thought, "they could work out their problems with their two kids." But then Dunn recalled how his own teenage daughter had nearly blown apart his second marriage – so he began a program to help stepfamilies stay together. Dunn's story is recounted in a book called *Marriage Savers*, written by Mike McManus.[9]

The article goes on to say that McManus notes that 65 percent of marriages involving stepchildren end up in divorce court. The only way for this tragic statistic to be reversed is for Christians to take a more proactive role in ministering to these families. It is easy for us to sit back in judgment or complacency when we don't feel involved. When we take ownership of the problem we are much more likely to support these families through prayer, counsel, and acts of service.

Disciplining your stepchildren

The Lord disciplines those he loves. Hebrews 12:6

Decisions about how to discipline the kids should be made long before you tie the knot. Sit down together and consider how you will handle a variety of circumstances and situations. What if your five-year-old steals a candy bar? How will you handle your teenager missing curfew? If your ten-year-old lies about schoolwork, what will you do?

This is just a tiny sampling of situations you are likely to face, sometimes on a daily basis. How do you plan to handle this? As a couple, you need to develop your strategy for survival. The first step is to each bring to the table the methods you used before. These may well be worlds apart. Discuss, pray, and reach an agreement on how to handle the situations as they come up. Decide who will administer the discipline and how it will be done. Initially, it may be best for you to discipline your own children, especially if they are adolescents. Once a relationship with your stepchildren grows stronger, both parents should be able to do it.

Recognize that sometimes you will be caught off guard. Agree now that you will not react to an unexpected situation until you have had time to talk and pray privately about what to do.

McManus warns stepparents to expect to be tested right away.

> During the couple's courtship, their children often get along well with both the prospective stepparent and stepsiblings...But that initial friendliness often disappears the moment the rice is thrown. Kids learn how to drive the stepparent up the wall. Often the child will do this without the natural parent catching on. Sometimes, the stepparent lacks the skills to deal effectively with the new spouse's children. Before the newlyweds know it, their lovely new family has morphed into the Brady Bunch from Hell. And they have no idea how to cope with the crisis.[10]

Children quickly learn to play one parent against the other. After being a single parent for some time, you may be used to making all the decisions. Without thinking, you may respond "yes" or "no" when a child makes a request. You can no longer do this if you want to remain sane. Kids who don't get the answer they want will often make the same request to the other parent. Some actually delight in causing conflicts because it gives them a feeling of power. So agree now to put important requests on hold until you two can confer. "Second marriages usually fail because of conflict over the discipline of the children," says Dr. Beth Brown. "For a stepfamily to find stability and happiness you must stand together."[11]

The best way to create that atmosphere of stability is to always present a united front to the children. In his book *Becoming a Couple of Promise*, Kevin Leman stresses the importance of continued unity. "You and your spouse have got to decide from the outset to be in it for the long-haul – by blending first, with the most solid of bonds. The children will test you and see if you are 'one flesh.' If the children…know they cannot defeat you, they begin adding wonderful things to the marriage. Satan simply cannot defeat you when you stay united."[12] If you disagree with your spouse about a disciplinary issue, do so privately and work out the best agreement you can. Stop and pray for wisdom if you're stuck on an issue. When parents don't agree, they often end up arguing in front of the children about how to reprimand their bad behavior. This is a disaster. It invites the kids to keep driving a wedge between you. Be careful to watch your body language as you discipline. Children pick up signals from our eye contact, facial expressions, and body stance more than we think. These negative cues often speak louder than our words. Life is confusing enough for our children so don't send mixed signals in your discipline. Parents who are consistently firm and loving in their discipline give the children a sense of security.

One of the best things you can do as a couple with your stepchildren is to establish from the outset that you will not tolerate disrespect in the home, either in the way the children address one another or in the way they address you as parents. It grieves our hearts to think of all the times we've heard family members yell out hurtful, disrespectful things like: "You're not my dad, you can't make me!" "Get out. You don't belong here!" or "I hate you!" They may have good reason to feel hurt or angry, and you have to acknowledge and address that. But it has to be done in an atmosphere of love and respect. The first time a child responds disrespectfully, you or your mate must calmly and firmly remind them of the already-stated consequences of such disrespect and quickly discipline them for it. You model respect by listening to the kids and your spouse when they speak, evaluating what they say, even if you may disagree with it. We have found rules without relationship lead to rebellion. So work hard at building relationships with your stepchildren or grandchildren. Seize every chance to build a relationship with them.

In our book *Raising Kids Right in a World Gone Wrong*, we stress the need for parents to deal quickly with anger in the home and model repentance and forgiveness. "Many a relationship has ended because someone did not deal with the anger felt toward another. The anger was buried inside until finally its poison seeped out, marring and destroying the relationship." The flip side of the anger issue is when families teach that it's okay to be angry and blow off steam at one another in the home. This will produce a volatile atmosphere where hurtful things are said and excused too easily. The best way to deal with the anger issue is to keep short accounts with one another. If a flare-up occurs, bring the offenders together to talk it out, reviewing what was said, and bringing the two to repentance and forgiveness.

One teenaged girl we interviewed said, "I was so angry over my parents' divorce. I stuffed a lot of it, but it sometimes came out in short, angry outbursts. I resented my new stepmom at first, but she helped me a lot. When I'd get mad she'd stop what she was doing and say, 'You don't need to yell. I am listening.' Then she really would listen. Usually I was upset about something that had happened that day, but the root of it was stuff from the divorce. Over time she helped draw that hurt out of me."

One stepfather figured out that there were more than thirty different two-person relationships in his new blended family of six children. "Working with this many complex relationships has been very difficult for both us and the kids. There have been a lot of flare-ups. There aren't simple answers for building a united family out of six wounded kids. You have to keep working at loving and understanding each one and building a sense of family stability and security. One thing that helps is to study personality types, birth order and the various phases of childhood."

Security is a huge issue for children in a second marriage. They have watched a marriage dissolve either through death or divorce. And the unpleasant reality is that it could happen again. No guarantee you make will cause them to feel totally secure. You build that sense of security by teaching them to put their trust in the Lord (who will never leave or forsake them), by loving them unconditionally (just as the Lord loves us), and by establishing and following clear boundaries for life (just as He has with us). As the kids feel more secure about your love for one another, for God, and for them, they will be able to feel secure in your discipline. Remember that some may still harbor feelings of guilt that they somehow contributed to the divorce or the parent's death because of their bad behavior. Some may wrongly feel that God is punishing them. By modeling the Father heart of God you will teach them that just isn't true.

Consistency is such a key aspect of this. Our heavenly Father is so consistently faithful in His love and discipline of us. If we are consistent in our love and discipline, our kids and stepchildren will likewise feel safe within the boundaries we set.

Whose church do we attend?

...that you and I may be mutually encouraged by each other's faith.
—Romans 1:12

This can be another emotional hot button in the process of blending two families. Hopefully, you both will have attended one another's home church a few times before you marry, and have started making friends in both places. It will be especially helpful to draw your teenagers into this decision. This demonstrates to them that you want to hear their opinion, and gives you an opportunity to pray about the decision as a family.

Uprooting kids from their friends and familiar surroundings may be devastating for some, while others take it in stride. In blending kids from two families and two churches, you probably won't be able to meet everyone's needs or desires. However, you can demonstrate to each that you want to reach the best possible decision by the way you listen and respond. If they are in a youth group or Sunday school that seems more concerned about social events than discipleship, this may be just the right opportunity to move them to a place where they will be challenged spiritually. But if your kids are already in a strong youth group, try not to move them.

Pete and Helen, a second-marriage couple, had to deal with the "church move" issue soon after they married. Pete's son Mark was sixteen at the time, and Helen's son Mike was fourteen. Because of his job, the family moved to the area where Pete lived, and they bought a new home. Their new home was a long drive from Pete and Mark's church so they decided to find a new one that would be closer and give a fresh start for their new family. They spent several months looking for that right church, and none seemed like a good fit for the boys. Mark, especially, could not adjust, no matter where they went.

Pete and Helen had spent much time praying and discussing the problem, but had not involved the boys in this process. They later realized their mistake, and they called a family meeting. Both boys shared openly about how they felt and they all prayed together for an answer. The family finally decided to return to Pete's old church, at least for a few years, because of the youth group there. Mark loved being back with old friends and a youth leader he respected, and he helped Mike find new friends. Soon both the boys were doing well. Sometimes we just need to go the second mile for our children.

When a move involves changing church denominations, or switching to a much larger or smaller congregation, take time with the kids and discuss the most apparent differences that will happen because of the change. Explain as best you can any distinctions in doctrine, worship style, church structure, etc. and affirm both churches. Invite questions and talk through with the kids the importance of knowing God personally and respecting the differences in how sincere Christians of other denominations or countries may worship Him.

In our situation it made sense for us to go to Duane's church because of the distance to mine. I accepted this willingly, but it meant leaving the denomination I'd been in all my life and friends I had known for many years. If your husband or wife or children are shy, this transition can be a long and lonely process. Help them by drawing them together with people they might build friendships with. And if the distance allows it, return to your spouse's former church occasionally for special services, weddings, and other social events to maintain old friendships and help ease the transition.

Michelle's two teenage boys, who had grown up in a conservative church connected with their ethnic origins, found it strange to attend the large charismatic church of their new stepfather. They attended grudgingly at first, but eventually prevailed on the parents to let them go back to their old church. This decision eased some family tensions, but it ultimately heightened the division within the blended family. Each couple must prayerfully settle this issue in their own hearts. Forcing headstrong teenagers to attend a new church may cause them to become resentful, but it might also lead them into new and potentially healthier relationships. Letting them go back to where they are comfortable may be the best for their stability and spiritual growth, but it could also be a subtle attempt on their part to divide the family and keep you from being more in touch with their spiritual development.

Gary and Shirley, two divorced people from California, merged two children from previous marriages when they married, and eventually had two daughters together. "If there was anything we did right, it was to find a good church and stay in fellowship with other believers," said Gary. "I don't even like to think of what might have happened had we not done that. What held our marriage and family together was believing in God, knowing that He hates divorce, and being connected to others who helped us make right choices even when we didn't particularly feel like it."

There is simply no substitute for having your children become part of a larger spiritual family that loves and affirms them, that supports your parental values, and models for them the ways of God. The church can be your greatest ally in this difficult journey. Look for a church with pastors, youth leaders, elders, and members who see themselves as a family and welcome you as part of it.

How do we handle holidays?

This is a day you are to commemorate; for the generations to come you shall celebrate… —Exodus 12:14

Holidays should be celebrations, not complications. But in a second marriage, you can expect lots of holiday complications. Before you marry, try to sort out how you might solve the particular issues surrounding your future holiday celebrations.

Christmas and Thanksgiving are the two most family-oriented and emotionally charged holidays. People routinely gather family and friends from near and far to feast together and celebrate in their own special ways. The bittersweet memories of holidays past and the complexities of new relationships and traditions often turn this happy season into a minefield of emotions. You can diffuse some of it with planning, but some problems can only be diffused by the grace of God.

If your children came out of a divorce you likely will have to divide holiday times with your ex or his or her parents. Making this an emotional tug of war every year can be incredibly hurtful to both children and adults. So if this scheduling can be done well beforehand, it will be less difficult for all concerned. These holidays are times when divorced parents are tempted to use the children to retaliate for past offenses. One mother told us, "My pride and anger wanted to keep the children for myself and have them love me alone. Somehow the Holy Spirit let me know that if I took the step of dividing father and child, my life could be filled with bitterness, which can become a deep, ugly root in your life. Hard as it was I had to live out Ephesians 4:31, which says, "Get rid of all bitterness, rage and anger … forgiving each other, just as in Christ God forgave you."

In a blended family there are now four sets of grandparents instead of two, and how close they are emotionally and physically will often play a major role in the holiday dynamics. If your family chooses to celebrate with extended family, it's common to alternate years (this year with my family, next year with yours) or the holidays themselves (Thanksgiving with my family, Christmas with yours).

Along the way, it's good to start forming your own family traditions. Dr. Beth Brown, who is a stepparent herself, suggests that these changes be made slowly. "I found that new traditions that did not compete with old ones were best. Instead of threatening family history, I added to it. … [My husband] Don remembers that before I came into the family, he used to put up the Christmas tree alone. After we were married I instituted a tree-trimming party and tree-trimming became a celebrated tradition in my new family."[13]

LeeAnn remember the first Christmas they had together just a month after they were married. Without thinking it through, they decided it would be good to gather both sides of the family at their large mountain home. LeeAnn's expectations were high. She hoped they could be one happy family. Well, she found she was wrong. It wasn't that they had an ugly scene or that they left unhappy with one another. It was just too soon to blend their families.

It seems the Smuckers have their traditions and the Rawlins, theirs. So they decided that from then on, at least for Christmas, they would have a Smucker Christmas and a Rawlins Christmas. It has worked well for them. They have LeeAnn's boys and families for Christmas Eve day brunch each year and for years, they had Christmas morning with the Rawlins. Things have changed a bit because some of Duane's children have moved away from them but they still try to have a time when they celebrate with both sides. You must do what works for your family.

The Smyth family from Michigan had to make several adjustments to cope with their divorce-related holiday issues. "Since the children spent Christmas with their other parents, we celebrated Christmas prior to their departure," said Vicki. "We exchanged names among the seven of us, making the surprise of who had whose name a big deal as one at a time we opened the other's gift. Richard and I didn't want materialism to be the focus of this important holiday. Also, we knew the children would be receiving lavish gifts from our former spouses and we chose not to compete with similar gifts. Our tradition centered on exchanging homemade goodies, playing carols, and remembering the real reason for the season. Now that our children are adults living in other cities, the name exchange is a tradition we still practice across the miles today."

"In the early years, the ex-grandparents caused many an upset by sending gifts to only three children," said Vicki. "This was solved easily as the Lord showed me to get the other two similar gifts. Sometimes we would just put a large bowl on the table and all the goodies went into it. Then everyone enjoyed whatever was sent."

Obviously, the holiday issue can't be resolved in the same way for everyone. But one thing every second-marriage person can do is to ask God to help you lay down your expectations for your version of a "happy holiday." When we put our expectations on others, we set ourselves up for unhappy holidays. To those without expectations, every good thing that happens is a gift.

Several of the stepparents we interviewed suggested celebrating new holidays that weren't celebrated much in the previous marriages – like Valentine's Day, July 4th, sports-related events, community events, etc. One stepmom makes a big event of every child's birthday. "It's a way of personally affirming each one and pulling us together as a family. They all seem to like it." As a stepparent you have to do the best you know how for your new family, and trust God to bring the result He wants from it.

LeeAnn is still working through the issue of feeling responsible for making everyone happy at holidays and birthdays. All her life she tried to make everyone in their family happy, even though she knew deep down it was impossible. It was very frustrating for her until God showed her something that is so simple, yet so profound. He taught her that it is not her place to bring happiness, for each of us holds the key to our own happiness and contentment. She found that her part is to bring His joy into every situation. Joy comes from the heart, and the heart is made pure by laying down your rights, by surrendering your will to God. In this incident, the issue for her was laying down the right for them to be one big happy family over the holidays. So if this is a problem for you ask God to reveal to you how you can change. Let Him change others, and you focus on your own heart.

Chapter 9

FINANCES IN A SECOND MARRIAGE

Y OU CAN USUALLY PREDICT the hottest issues in a second marriage. Just think about what's closest to your heart. For many couples, money ranks second only to children as a source of conflict. There can be all kinds of "flash points," and you would do well to work through them before tying the knot. Look ahead to the implications of merging your accounts, repaying debt, and selling properties. Discuss your spending habits, questions of who will manage the finances, potential job changes and divorce-related issues like child support and alimony. Ask hard questions about your future spouse's attitudes toward giving, budgeting, and investing for the future. Does he or she seem controlling and secretive about money? Does he or she recognize God's lordship in their finances? Does your prospective spouse seem contented or is he or she always looking for some new purchase or investment? These are important clues to financial values.

Applying God's principles

Applying God's principles to your finances can make a huge difference in the ultimate success of your marriage. The acclaimed Crown Ministries financial stewardship program notes that Jesus said more about money than any other subject. In all there are 2,350 verses related to finances in the Bible. This begs the question of why so many. Crown leaders note that it's because Jesus knew that how we handle money impacts our fellowship with the Lord, that it competes with the Lord for mastery of our lives, and because so much of life revolves around the use of money.[14]

Sadly, many Christians make little effort to apply this time-tested wisdom. We may not see it in ourselves, but we often get swept up in rampant materialism so prevalent in Western society. More than one slender, wealthy woman has been credited with the observation, "One can never be too thin or too rich." And that's how many of us live, buying the lie that more is always better. The media fuels our runaway consumerism with constant appeals to our pride, greed, insecurities, and lusts. And if we don't have the money for something we want, we can just reach for the plastic. Buy now. Pay later. No down payment. Easy terms. No wonder we've become a nation of credit card junkies!

How often people going into second marriages attempt to use money to fulfill their dreams and visions only to discover the hollowness of its material pleasures. Whenever one spouse looks to the other to be their financial security, it places their trust in money (and another human being) rather than in God. We've found that even people with lots of money struggle with issues of security. Fear of failure and loss of their cherished possessions seems to consume many of them. They find themselves anxious, unable to sleep, and overburdened by the energy needed to protect, repair, care for, and pay for their possessions.

"About 80 percent of our waking day is consumed in thinking about money: making it, saving it, spending it, or giving it away," according to the late Larry Burkett, a Christian financial expert and author of *The Complete Financial Guide for Young Couples*. That's why it is so important to have clear understanding of your future spouse's financial attitudes and practices as you enter into a second marriage. Inevitably there will be some differences in your values. Each of you grew up in different homes, and your life experiences shaped the views you now have. You don't have to agree on everything, but you should agree on the important things.

How we give

It's always been important to LeeAnn that her husband be a generous giver. As a child, her father taught her the joy of giving, and her first husband was also a generous man. It could have been a major source of conflict in her second marriage if she had married someone who was stingy and selfish. Thankfully, God gave her another husband who loves to give, and she is so glad she discovered that before marriage. If you find yourself married to someone who does not share your financial priorities, get help from a godly counselor. Whatever you do, do not nag. Nagging only brings anger and is of no help at all. Be kind and gentle. Talk to God. He is a great listener and loves to give us the desires of our hearts. Encourage your spouse to pray with you about financial issues, and seek the counsel of the Scriptures when you come to an issue you don't understand.

Facing financial crises

Our friend Thomas who told us, "We have had several financial crises in our marriage, but each was really just a test of faith. I've found that the best way to handle our finances is to pray together about our needs. At one time we were $45,000 in credit card debt. On our own, we were making no headway; the interest was eating up the entire payment. We panicked about what to do. Praying together gave us incredible peace in those times. Again and again, the Lord showed Himself faithful when we presented our needs to Him and stayed true to the principles He was teaching us about tithing, avoiding further debt, being honest with creditors and faithfully paying our bills."

Thomas' wife told us, "God led us to a consumer credit counseling service, and they helped us work out a plan. Best of all, they were able to negotiate with the credit card companies so our balances had a simple and often, much lower interest. Without compounding interest, we watched our balances go down steadily. Today we are debt-free. We only wish we had done it years earlier, but we let pride and fear that we'd lose our good credit rating hold us back. What a lie! Since I am more gifted in math than Thomas, I handle most of the budgeting and bill paying, but we work together on financial planning and taxes. It has to be a partnership."

We feel that both the lack of money or abundance of it can cause division between a husband and wife. If you are willing to let God work on your hearts He will actually use money to draw you closer together. The choice, as always, is up to you.

You may recall that a key item on my list of qualities in a new wife was that she have money. I thought that both of us having money would make it easier, and I didn't want a woman who was attracted to me because of my wealth. Little did I realize that by marrying a woman of means that I would be assuming a good deal of responsibility for managing her estate. It's been nice to have the freedom that such wealth brings, but finances have also been one of our larger areas of conflict.

Since we each have children from our first marriages, we felt it would work best to keep our estates separate, in part for their sakes. We set up new accounts, while our home and a number of things are in a combined ownership. So we have things that are ours, some that are hers, and some that are mine. Needless to say, this requires careful communication about how finances are managed and what is communicated to others. My wife desires to keep our financial circumstances as private as possible. This creates a bit of a problem when she marries a man who considers his life an open book. I've learned to be respectful of my spouse's concerns and to view ourselves as stewards of the resources God has placed in our care.

As we have grown older and truly become one, we have attempted to simplify our lives and give ourselves to things that have the greatest eternal value. When the funeral home staff took away my beloved wife for the last time, I saw so clearly how unimportant "things" really are. Betty's lovely dresses and expensive jewelry meant nothing. LeeAnn's experience in losing her husband Willard was similar. She saw how truly rich he was in the 1,500 friends who came to this humble Oregon farmer's memorial service. What really counts for eternity is the treasure we store up in heaven through loving relationships here on earth.

Several years into our marriage we sat down with some friends and asked them to help us sort out this area of our marriage. It proved to be quite helpful. I am not sure we learned all that much from our friends, but they provided a neutral listening ear as we talked to each other. Here are some of the things we did that helped:

1. We committed to making all major financial decisions together and to keep open communication.

2. We set up a bank account that we both put money into each month. Then we pay our regular bills out of that account.

3. We also set up a 501 (C) 3 nonprofit charitable corpo-

ration, and we each use it to meet charitable needs.

4. We loan monies back and forth to each other as needed in our businesses. We try to keep this as clean as we can with good records.

5. When we encounter difficulties we seek help from a friend. It is much easier for someone from the outside to offer objective solutions.

Keep in mind that all that we have belongs to the Lord. Hold things loosely! The older we get, the more clearly we see the truth of Christ's words in Mark 8:38, "What good is it for a man to gain the whole world, yet forfeit his soul?" God gives us blessings to enjoy. Don't ruin that blessing with selfishness and greed. Remember, the way you handle financial problems is a good indicator of whether or not you trust God.

The financial baggage of divorce is well known. "Divorce often creates additional problems and pain that had formerly not existed, such as child custody, support payments, and heartbreak," says Chris L. Stollar in an article for the Focus on the Family's Web site www.family.org.

This truth plays out daily in the second marriages of millions of Americans. Consider this scenario: A divorced man pays a third of his net income in court-ordered child support for his two sons who live out of state with their mother. When the man marries a divorced woman with two children of her own, he inherits financial responsibility for them, too, because their deadbeat dad is a year behind in child support. This father has the additional costs of airfare for flying his own sons home for holidays and summer visitation times. He works longer hours trying to earn more to keep his family afloat, and ultimately he sees them less and less. All this is a recipe for family stress and financial disaster, yet it happens over and over again.

Sometimes grandparents or in-laws can cause problems for parents by either giving money or buying things that are inappropriate and not in keeping with the parents' desires for their child. We know of one grandfather who bought a pickup truck for his grandchild against the better judgment of the parents. This created a huge problem because the young man was not ready to be responsible or own a truck of his own. The grandson felt it was his truck, and he could do as he pleased. The grandfather felt pity for his grandson because of his parents' divorce and was trying to somehow make up for it. Truth is, it only made matters worse. It caused a rift in the entire family. It would have been far better if the grandfather had sat down with the parents and worked out some form of trust that could have been used at a later date when the grandson was more mature and could really use the financial help.

Those seeking to remarry need to crunch the numbers of their joint finances before making the decision to go to the altar again. This is a time for stark honesty. If your outlays for alimony, child support, old debts, back taxes, etc. make it impossible to make ends meet in a monthly budget, then you are only fooling yourself if you think you will make it in a second marriage.

Most married couples plan their wedding with greater care than they plan their financial strategies. Could this be why surveys peg money problems as the No. 1 cause of divorce?

Some of the strategies that should be discussed are:

1. Do either of you have a bad credit record?
2. Have either of you filed bankruptcy in the past?
3. How much credit card debt does either of you have?
4. How about school debt?
5. How about health care debts?

These are just some questions we should ask each other before we marry to avoid problems afterwards.

Bill and Shirley found it a good idea to set aside some time periodically to talk about financial issues. This helped them avoid problems, and they did not have to spend their leisure time talking about money issues.

One divorced father in St. Louis fell in love with a single mother he met at a church singles group. After the two were engaged, she confessed to him that she had a problem with credit card debt. She assured him that she had changed, and he began to help her in hopes of easing her financial burdens. But she hid from him her continuing use of credit cards. Soon she began manipulating him emotionally, begging for his help to pay overdue rent and utility bills. She was draining his savings rapidly when a Christian counselor stepped in to urge him to break off the relationship. He did, but at great cost financially and emotionally.

We recommend that divorced singles intending to remarry sit down with a trusted financial counselor and lay out all their financial records, mapping out projected income and expenses in a monthly or annual budget. If your income is tight, we highly recommend that you live by a monthly budget. It helps you anticipate your needs and head off problems before they become crises.

How to develop a budget

There are numerous budgeting software packages on the market today, including Quicken, Microsoft Money, Task Manager, and Money Matters. Likewise, there are scores of budgeting books on the market. Any of these will work for you if you are committed to keeping track of your finances.

If you are disciplined enough to record your income and expenses regularly, we highly recommend using a budgeting software program. It will help you to easily track your spending habits, categorize items to create simple reports, and help you with taxes. If computers scare you then a simple ledger book will do.

1. Start tracking – The first thing to do in setting up a budget is to track your spending for one to three months. Record everything you bring in and everything you spend.

2. Analyze your expenses – When you're done with this recording time, analyze your spending to see how it falls into certain categories such as tithes or offerings, taxes, savings, housing, food, utilities, insurances, car expenses, credit cards, entertainment, gifts, clothing and personal items.

3. Anticipate income – If you have regular paychecks or income, note the payday on one page of your budget book. Estimate the amount of income you will receive during that period.

4. Record your regular expenses – Align your bills to these paydays, making sure that you have ample time for checks to arrive on time through the mail. Consider paying bills online or through an automatic bill pay system offered by most banks.

These are some suggestions that can help you work through this hard issue. But if we can remember to go to God's word for help we will be more successful in overcoming or avoiding these problems.

Money can be a wedge that drives us apart as couples, but it does not have to be. Money problems can be an opportunity for a couple to understand each other better, strengthen their unity, and learn to work together better. We read in Proverbs some wonderful guidelines from God to help us with this issue.

Proverbs 1:7: "The fear of the Lord is the beginning of wisdom."

Proverbs 16:3: "Commit to the Lord whatever you do, and your plans will succeed."

Chapter 10

GROWING OLD
GRACEFULLY TOGETHER

*Grow old along with me, the best is yet to be, the last of life,
for which the first was made.* —*Robert Browning*

WE LOVE THIS Robert Browning quotation. It states so well how we feel about getting old together. In modern-day language it is said like this: "Have a blast while you last."

Often in a second marriage we are older and are looking for someone with whom we can spend our senior years. This opens another area we need to consider when we remarry.

We have discovered that as we grow older we want doors to open in a hurry; it seems time is running out. We are glad that to God, age does not mean a whole lot. He never seems to be in a hurry. In His Word He talks a lot about waiting and resting, both of which are easier for us now that we are older.

In Psalm 71:18 the psalmist desired to pass along his understanding of the Lord to others, and he prayed, "When I am old and gray headed, O God do not forsake me, until I declare your strength to this generation." This is what we are writing about in this chapter. We need to remain open to how we can be used by God in our senior years. We have much to give; and remember, in giving we receive.

Senior years

Some say we are now over the hill. I guess that means from now on it is all down hill. Of course it goes without saying, everything seems to move faster. Birthdays come every few months, it seems. In fact, they are coming so fast, we have decided to stop having them.

As we mature we are realizing, perhaps for the first time, that we are becoming the person we always wanted to be. Of course we are a long way from perfect but hopefully we are much better than we were twenty years ago. We look in the mirror and wonder who that old person is staring back at us. The wrinkles, silver hair, and aching bones cause us to despair but this despair does not last long.

We would never trade our walk with Jesus, or our wonderful walk with each other, our amazing friends, and all the other rich gifts God has given us for less gray hair or a flatter tummy. Besides, our society makes far too much about how we look. It is what is in our heart that counts.

As we age, we have become kinder to ourselves and each other and much less critical. The little bumps in the road do not bother us nearly as much.

It has been nineteen years since we were wed in Hawaii and we are still very much in love. Oh yes, we sometimes forget things. We have to work much harder at keeping track of our keys, bills and correspondence but that's okay. Some of life is just as well forgotten. We eventually remember the important things. Our focus these days is on things with eternal value.

Reflecting back

As we reflect back on our courtship days we realize how important it was that we were very selective about whom we were to marry. It is like most everything in life. If you are very careful and select only items with high quality, that are well put together, they will last longer. We believe our marriage has been wonderful, not only because we have worked at it, but also because we were very well suited to live together because of our common faith and similar view of life.

It has also helped a great deal to sit down and agree upon a set of values or principles that we choose to live by and our willingness to be accountable to each other for living them out on a daily basis. We realize because of our uniqueness they may be different from what others think are important, but they work for us and that's what counts. Find out what works for you.

Finding our strengths

In the process of growing old together we have come to understand how important it is to first learn each other's strengths. One thing that did help us was to take a Clifton Strength Finder test. This test can be found in the book *Now, Discover Your Strengths* by Marcus Buckingham and Donald O. Clifton. This book helps us bring high achievement and happiness in exercising our strengths, instead of focusing on correcting our weaknesses.

Of course with these different motivations, we each have had to learn to die to our expectations. This allowed us to give each other space to be who God called us to be instead of living up to certain expectations we had for each other. Little by little we have learned to let God change the other person and then we do our best to accept the person just the way he or she is.

Each year we learn to be more flexible and less demanding of each other. Yes, we have learned an important lesson – we have earned the right to be wrong, admit it and get on with life.

Focusing on the positive

Perhaps it is a part of who we are but as we grow in our acceptance, we are learning to be more positive. Over the years we have realized how harmful it is to our unity when we focus on each other's flaws. It only seems to bring out the worst in us. So we have begun to focus on all the great qualities we see in each other. We have decided to be as blind as possible in seeing each other's faults and, believe it or not, they seem to drop off and become unimportant.

Not long ago some friends shared this story with us. Let's call them Sam and Grace. Grace loved getting gifts. Giving and receiving gifts was part of her love language. Sam discovered this and started buying her things. Instead of being grateful, Grace was often not happy with what he had chosen for her. It did not fit, it was the wrong color, or she just did not like his selection. Grace often returned what he had purchased for her. She never seemed grateful. It was not long till Sam stopped buying her gifts. Grace focused on what she received (the gift) and not the kindness of the giver.

Be careful what you focus on. Remember to look at the heart as Jesus does. It would have been so much kinder if Grace had sat down with Sam and shared her heart. Even if he did miss it sometimes, any gift is better then no gift at all.

A few years back someone said you will find joy when you put Jesus first, others second, and yourself last. We no longer try to make each other happy but seek ways to bring joy into our lives and the lives of others. This has especially helped LeeAnn because one of her strengths that can become a weakness is trying to make everyone happy. It was great when one day during her quiet time, God said, "LeeAnn, it is not your job to make everyone happy. It is your job to bring joy to others." This may seem small but there is a lot of difference in trying to cause a grumpy person to become happy versus giving a cup of cold water to a thirsty child.

Fidelity

It is very comforting to know that our mate is absolutely trustworthy. It is also comforting to know our mate is totally committed to marriage until parted by death. Trust and confidence come when we remain faithful to each other. It's comforting to never be jealous or fearful about whether or not we are loved and honored by our mate.

It is very disturbing to us to watch older couples constantly correcting each other, never completely trusting their mate's judgment or agreeing with what their mate says. Maybe it is a habit we get into or maybe it's just being old and crotchety. However, this is no excuse. Be loving and kind to each other. It is so beautiful to watch older couples love and cherish each other.

. Not long ago in a writing class we attended, one of the older gentlemen wrote this about his wife of fifty some years. It touched our hearts so much we asked him if we might include it here.

> She strode toward us from the shadows into the sun, like a starlet finding the spotlight. Then came that million-dollar smile. She held it for the last five steps. Was she amused? Did she know what she was doing to me? I dropped my car keys. In picking them up, my eyes moved slowly past her chalk-white sneakers, up those honey-tanned, shapely legs, and snow-white shorts. I closed and opened in a slow blink as I came to the

red and white striped blouse. I wondered, *did the designer delib-
erately arrange those stripes to accentuate the positive?* I was sixteen,
you know.

Soft flowing waves of golden blonde surrounded her per-
fectly sculpted face. The spotlight sun haloed that hair and the
effect left me speechless.

Then came that smile. I've never been the same.

Isn't that beautiful? We know this couple well and all these
years later he still sees her as he did some fifty years ago. That is
what we mean about love lasting on and on. This is the beauty of
love even in our senior years.

One day in Hawaii, LeeAnn was having coffee with a friend
and watching the beautiful waves hit the shore. They were talking about their men, as ladies often do. Her friend, who is also
in her senior years, said the sweetest thing about her husband of
many years "Oh, I love him so much and when he walks in the
room my stomach still churns." Love does go on forever if we
nurture it.

The one thing

Not only is it refreshing for older couples to display love for
each other, it is also rewarding to watch older couples who truly
have a shared purpose in life, even in their senior years.

It has taken us a long time to find the one thing that matters
most to us as a couple. Jesus made it clear when He gave us the
greatest commandment. He stated in Luke 10:27: "You shall love
the Lord your God with all your heart, and with all your soul,
and with all your strength, and with all your mind, and your
neighbor as yourself."

This needed to be personalized in our lives. It all boiled down to this. We want to be vessels of love to everyone we meet. This brought us to our decision to focus on children at risk. We are not sure what all of this will entail, but our desire is to be available where needed. This may well require a variety of actions on our part. The great thing is that we are in this together. We are constantly looking for ways to support each other's dreams and actions. A wonderful truth is that we will not fail in this activity as long as we refuse to give up.

Look for opportunities to serve

A few years ago we bought a home in Palm Springs, California, to spend the winters. We enjoyed it for a while but one can only shop and golf so much. We longed to do things that had eternal value. So we sold our place and bought in Kona, Hawaii, where the University of the Nations (Youth With A Mission) is located. We found we could volunteer at the university and work with students from all over the world. It is a wonderful experience and very fulfilling. The University has a website YWAM.org or UofNKona.edu. Check it out for many opportunities available for those in their senior years. We looked for things we love doing together and looked for places where we could serve. Ask the Lord to help find just the right place. Look for places that are best suited to your gifts. There are many places in need of retired (or re-fired) seniors to volunteer. We truly are fulfilled as we work together as much or as little as we please. Being active helps us to focus less on the aches and pains of growing old.

Enjoying grandparenting

Our grandchildren have brought us great joy. Together we have fifteen wonderful grandchildren. Each one is unique and very special to us. We want to leave a legacy for them. This may include a certain amount of financial support but we are mostly interested in modeling a godly life and marriage. We want to show them the importance of living lives that honor God while keeping eternal values as a high priority. It is very important to us to leave in our children's and grandchildren's hearts a deep love for God's Word. This is so important to us that not long ago we got an idea from some friends to help us establish this in their hearts. We gave the older ones a Walk Through The Bible. In this Bible we put a note that said we would pay them for reading this Bible each day till they had finished reading through it. That year most of them took our challenge and finished reading all the way through, some got part way. We are not sure if this helped them establish a habit of spending more time in the Word or not. We do know they know it was important enough to us to make this investment.

We want to show our grandchildren how to grow old grace-fully. It is our desire to not only show them how to live but how to finish the race.

It is wonderful that we are not directly responsible for teaching our grandchildren, as we were when we were raising our children. However, we do enjoy the input we have in their lives.

Just last summer Duane took two of our grandchildren, Matt, sixteen; Mark, fourteen; and a friend of Mark's, also fourteen, on a mission trip to Mexico. As they drove down to Mexico they took time to stop at an amusement park and have fun together. They went to an orphanage, where they painted rooms, fixed fences, scrubbed floors, and did a number of other jobs together.

In their free time they played soccer with the Mexican children. In the evenings they would spend time worshiping and sharing stories. It was a wonderful experience for them. They created memories and bonded together in a way they will never forget. Duane said, "It was the highlight of my summer."

Grandkids camp

Some friends gave us the idea of having a "Grandkids Camp" with their grandchildren. We loved the idea and decided to have one for our grandkids. We have a home in the mountains that we go to each summer. For the past few years we have conducted "Grandkids Camps" there. We make this their time, doing special activities just with them. We do things like having quiet times with them, trying to teach them how important we feel it is to have that time each day with the Lord. Poppie takes the boys to hit golf balls, or ride bikes and Nannie spends time with the girls, teaching them to do crafts, going to the soda fountain to enjoy a smoothie together, or maybe splashing in the pool. There are all kinds of things we can do – play games, read, go on treasure hunts, or put a puzzle together, just to name a few. Get creative and find out what they enjoy and do that. Be young and silly again – they love it. The little ones love to jump in our bed and snuggle with us, laughing and giggling. What fun it is to have several days together with them. These memories are priceless to us and to the grandkids.

There are many ways you can grandparent; as we said, be creative. We have found the best thing we can give them is our time and attention. The beauty of this is that as we grow older, we have more time to give to them. So spend time and share with them, they truly are a special gift.

If for some reason you do not have your own grandchildren,

or yours do not live near you, adopt some. There are many children out there that would love to have the love and attention from a grandparent. It will be a blessing to both them and you.

Removing the fear of death

We want to show our grandchildren how to live life and how to die. No one wants to talk about death these days, but as we move into this final season of our lives, we think it is healthy to talk about death, heaven, and eternal values. We choose to talk about how we can face and overcome this common fear of dying. As Christians, we are convinced that death is merely a door to a new, exciting wonderful life. We plan to enjoy that new life with God, His son Jesus, and our family and friends that have gone on before us. A very high calling for us is to pray daily that all our children and grandchildren will choose to follow the Lord, which would result in our being able to spend eternity together.

BIBLIOGRAPHY

Brown, Beth E. *When You're Mom No. 2*. Ann Arbor MI: Servant Publications, 1991.

Cerling, Charles. *Remarriage: Opportunity to Grow*. Old Tappan NJ: Revell, 1988.

Cunningham, Loren. *Is That Really You, God?: Hearing the Voice of God*. Grand Rapids, MI: Chosen Books, 1984.

McManus, Mike. *Marriage Savers: Helping Your Friends and Family Stay Married*. Grand Rapids, MI: Zondervan.

Ogilvie, Lloyd John. *God's Best for My Life*. Eugene, Oregon: Harvest House, 1981.

Smoke, Jim. *Living Beyond Divorce*. Eugene OR: Harvest House, 1984.

FOOTNOTES

1. Loren Cunningham, *Is That Really You, God?: Hearing the Voice of God* (Grand Rapids, MI: Chosen Books, 1984), 155, 157.

2. Lloyd John Ogilvie, *God's Best for My Life* (Eugene, Oregon: Harvest House, 1981), 1.

3. Beth E. Brown, *When You're Mom No. 2* (Ann Arbor, MI: Servant Publications, 1991), 93.

4. Jim Smoke, *Living Beyond Divorce* (Eugene, OR: Harvest House, 1984), 70-71.

5. Charles Cerling, *Remarriage: Opportunity to Grow* (Old Tappan, NJ: Revell, 1988), 95.

6. Brown, 97.

7. Ralph Ranieri, *The Blended Family: Guide for Stepparents* (Ligouri, MO: Ligouri Publications, 1988), 11.

8. Michelle Pearson, *Speaking the Right Language* (www. parentingteens.com/stepfamilies).

9. From BreakPoint, 2002, Copyright © 2002 Prison Fellowship Ministries. "BreakPoint with Chuck Colson"

10. Mike McManus, *Marriage Savers: Helping Your Friends and Family Stay Married* (Grand Rapids, MI: Zondervan).

11. Brown, 115.

12. Kevin Leman, *Becoming a Couple of Promise* (Colorado Springs: NavPress Publishing Group, 1999).

13. Brown, 104

14. Crown Ministries Small Group Financial Study (Longwood, FL: Crown Financial Ministries), 9-10.